The HUSTlER'S HolyBooK

THE HUSTLER'S HolyBook

GIVEN TO YOU BY
THE HUSTLAFARIANS

Published by Hustlafari

First published in the UK in 2015 by Hustlafari

ISBN 978-0-9933654-0-9

GOD LOVES A HUSTLER

CONTENTS

INTRODUCTION

EPILOGUE

INTRODUCTION

The dictionary describes a hustler as, '*A person who is good at aggressive selling or dishonest dealing.*'

Times have changed and with it so has the meanings of certain words. A hustler is someone who can make something out of nothing and this does not always mean in an illegal or dishonest way. A true hustler can turn a pound into a thousand pounds, an idea into a product, and a product into a business. In this day and age, many *'hustlers'* are perfectly law-abiding citizens, and sometimes the only difference between a hustler and a businessman is a shirt and a tie.

There are those who claim to be a hustler from the very first time they make some money, but in reality they are far from. The intention of this book is to teach you about the financial world and show you some of the skills and qualities you will need to become a true hustler. However you make your income there are basic understandings you need to be aware of if you intend to conquer this world of money. There are folk stories of men who were famous for stealing from the rich and giving to the poor. Here in these pages the same has happened but only instead of stealing gold and other commodities, it is knowledge that has been acquired, and all of this will be shared with you.

Some say knowledge is priceless but the truth is everything has a price because everything has value. People's values differ but most people know the importance of knowledge and value it highly. Humans are constantly learning and the more knowledge one can obtain the more success one can achieve. Knowledge like treasure is often kept a secret by those who wish to be richer than others. If knowledge is treasure then hustlers are treasure seekers. But how can one find treasure without a map? **The Hustler's Holy Book** is a map. Its words, and the thoughts it will evoke, will lead you closer to the treasures you wish to find. But remember, map reading takes a certain skill. Not everything will be clear at first and there will be some ideas and terminology that you do not understand straight away. Study the book. Study the map. Only those who seek shall find.

CHAPTER 1

THE DEFINITION OF A HUSTLER

A hustler is someone who is ambitious, someone who is willing to put in hard work and take the necessary steps to achieve their goals. No obstacle can get in the way of a true hustler because they will always find a way around it. A hustler does not take days off because they enjoy what they do. Hustling is not a job title but a culture and a way of life. Like many things in the world, words are subject to change. The definition of the word hustler is a clear example of this. The word hustler recurs throughout this book so it is vital that to begin with you fully understand the definition of this word and its origin.

The word hustler means one who hustles. The word hustler first originated from the Dutch word '*husselen*' which means '*to shake*'. The Dutch played a game called '*hustle-cap*' and the word husselen meant '*to shake*' and '*to toss*', especially money in a cap as part of the game. After this time the word began to be used but with many different meanings.

TIMELINE

1684 – To shake or to toss

1751 – A shaking movement meaning to push roughly or to shove

1812 – To hurry or to move quickly

1825 – In American English, a thief

1840 – To obtain in a quick illegal manner

1882 – In the sense of an energetic person, especially a salesman

1887 – In American English, to sell goods aggressively

1924 – In the sense of a prostitute

1963 – The noun sense of illegal business activity

The dictionary and thesaurus have failed to update with the times. Beside the word hustler should read '*ambitious*', '*hard – working*', '*entrepreneur*', '*money – maker*' and many more positive titles and descriptions.

21st century - A hustler is simply someone who makes money for themselves legally or illegally. Some people might dispute the former and believe only the latter, but it is just a matter of opinion and interpretation. If you are an entrepreneur, a businessman, anyone who grinds and puts in the hard graft for your money, then without a doubt you are a hustler.

CHAPTER 2

THE HUSTLER'S HISTORY

Before you know where you are going, you must know where you came from. So to better understand hustling you need to consider how it has been used historically. Throughout time, in every corner of the world, man has had to hustle as a form of survival. Even cavemen would have hustled each other to gain food, women or prominence. Therefore, it is useful to look back through history and examine the teachings of the people who have successfully done what you are trying to achieve before you. Could you be a Christian if you did not read the Bible and know about the life of Abraham, Moses and Jesus? Could you be a Muslim if you did not understand the prophet Mohammed and Allah's teachings? Could you be a Buddhist without understanding the four noble truths and the life of the Buddha? Get the point? Can you really call yourself a hustler if you do not know the great hustlers who came before you, the history of why people use

money to trade, and what has happened and is still happening, in the financial world? The simple answer is '*no*'. In this chapter you will learn some valuable information that will help you to continue hustling but now with a much clearer view of what it is all about.

The word money is of Latin origin. However, Romans did not invent money. It is important to understand that history has always been manipulated by whoever is in power. A book written in the West of the world will differ in facts from a book written in the East. A wise man once said history is just '*his story*'. Everybody's story is different. To delve into history is like finding treasure in the ocean. There is so much to explore. To get close to the truth one must gather stories from all corners of the world: from the scriptures of ancient Africa to the Middle Eastern scrolls and sacred teachings of the Asian Pacific; from knowledge handed down by holy men, passed on from generation to generation; from elders and scholars who teach the young and pass on their wisdom. When a father would teach his son how to survive and become a man, it would have been essential to school him on the unwritten laws of money. Different societies, cultures and civilizations all had different methods. One thing that stands out from all the scriptures and texts is an underlying need for survival. The ancient man did not measure each other by ones wealth. Strength and physical ability were more precious than any material or commodity. But that is not to say commodities were not important. A man with more was the envy of his fellow countrymen.

The actual word money is said to come from an inscription on a temple in Rome dedicated to one of the Roman's Gods called Juno. The Romans had many Gods and Juno Moneta was supposedly the queen of them all. The month June is named after her. She is also the God of matrons and marriage and this is a reason why traditionally many people have their weddings in June.

The inscription on the temple in Rome reads, "*Juno Moneta Regina*", literally translated as "*Juno, Queen of Warning*", the Latin *'Moneta'* meaning *'warning'* in the ancient Roman language. In 390 BC, under the cover of darkness, the Gauls attacked Rome. They had waited until all the watchmen and watchdogs were asleep but, as the story goes the sacred geese of Juno saw the Gauls and raised the alarm. The Romans were awakened and were able to defend Rome and fight off the attack. So, to honour Juno, the Romans built for her the temple of Capitoline Jupiter. The temple included a treasure house hidden inside at the back which contained gold, silver and bronze which were to be minted and sorted into coins. At this time, temples were still the safest places to house treasures as enemies still respected to a degree, places of worship.

The temple of Capitoline Jupiter was completed in 273BC and renamed Juno Moneta; Juno Queen of Warning, which later became Juno Queen of Money. The queen's face was printed on some of the coins and most coins would have had her name inscribed on them too. This did not sit well with everyone living within the Roman Empire. The Jews did not like using the Roman coinage, as it went against their religious beliefs having a Roman God on the coin face. Instead they would trade using a silver coin known as the half shekel. But the money lenders would charge interest on the half shekel and profit off of the Jews. Realising they were being extorted the Jews decided to start dealing in money themselves to give their people a better rate. Clearly the power was in the hands of those who controlled the money, something that has remained consistent throughout history.

Knowledge of history can give one a better understanding of current affairs. This knowledge allows one to understand, not only the changes that have occurred over time, but also what has remained the same. The descendants of Babylon still rule and the world still currently follows many Babylonian traditions such as the Babylonian calendar. This is very important to understand as a hustler because ancient philosophers knew the importance of the stars and the universe and their relationship with business. The moon cycle is 28 days. A calendar month should follow the moon cycle to give an accurate understanding of time and space, but the Babylonian people created a new calendar that used the sun and stars to calculate the years. For the average person who does not study astrology, this is hard to understand but as a hustler you must be aware that everything is relative. Many people, especially in the East of the world believe doing business on the wrong days can have bad consequences. Bank holidays are an example of bankers choosing specific days not to do business. It has also been said not to do business on a full moon but that a new moon is good for business. These ancient ideas must be studied. Understanding history will give one greater chances of success.

The story of money and banks is far older than the Juno Moneta story. History is never fixed or unchanging because it is always based on evidence available; and because new evidence can always be found, in turn, history changes. Different empires have risen over the years and since a means to travel was not easy in the past, different accounts of events were noted and spoken about but as they got passed around from here to there they got distorted; people will also have different truths and view the world in their own particular ways. Unholy men, that is, those who are unconscious or unaware, will always want to claim they discovered or invented whatever is important, so history may not be accurate if they are the ones telling it.

Because mankind is so divided people side to their roots, but wise men, the holy men, know different. In the early years of civilization man was one. Over the course of many years man spread across the world. Geography of the world has changed and the land on earth has moved. Indigenous people come from all corners of the world but the earliest civilizations come from the continent now known as Africa and this is accepted by the majority of philosophers, anthropologists and historians. Great kings in Africa ruled long before the empires of Rome. Archaeologists have discovered evidence of great cities where trade would have been ripe.

Asia was the next region in the world where empires rose. As humans spread across the world their thirst for knowledge and discovery grew, each civilization learning from the ones before them; man passing on his knowledge. This is why nobody can make claim to anything because with every invention, theory and discovery some knowledge had to have come from someone else. This affects the history of money; each system taking from the ones before up until this present time. The money lenders are now the bankers. A handful of men control the banks and set the value of money that is used all over the world. They can manipulate the financial market to suit them and the result is the world is currently in a position where the gap between the wealthy and poor continues to grow.

If the history of man starts in Africa then the history of money also starts here. Africa, which is named after one of her conquerors, is the second largest continent on earth. So some history has been lost and some history is open for interpretation as there is not always hard evidence to examine. Some people only trust what the eye can see but wise people know different. The reason for this is that man's true essence is spirituality. When someone is truly in touch with their own spirit there is no need for anything else. The early man knew this and the early man was content. There was no physical money and no need for money, but at a point in history things changed.

Early civilizations did not write things down as modern ones do; most knowledge was handed down orally. The elders would teach the young with stories and songs. The young would memorise these stories and songs and pass them on when they grew older to their own young and this is how it went on for thousands of years. Africa is still home to the most ancient civilizations. There are many tribes that still use stories to teach the young to this very day. This little story or *'his story'* (history) about to be told is an example of how knowledge was passed down and evidence of one of the earliest forms of hustling.

Oku woke up one morning. His father Bulu was revered as one of the chief elders in the village and people would often go to him for advice. On this bright and sunny morning, an old woman from the next village that was many miles away arrived at the front of Oku's house. Oku called to his father, *"Father there is a woman here to see you."* Bulu stopped what he was doing and came to see what the old woman wanted. She explained that she had been walking for miles and was thirsty, and so Oku collected some water for her on the instructions of his father. The old woman then told Bulu that she had heard of a man in a village beyond their own who could turn stone into water. The woman had with her a bag full of stones; stones that Bulu had come across himself. Now, these stones were probably what people know today as diamonds but back then in Oku's lifetime, in his village, water was considered far more precious, for water sustained life. Stones, however beautiful, were useless, and so a man who could turn stones into water was a very special man indeed. Bulu had to walk over a mile every day to get fresh water and so, naturally, the woman's claims intrigued him, for if he could turn stones into water he would not have to walk so far each morning. Bulu explained to his young son that he was going to set out with the old woman in the morning to go and find this man. At dawn, they left. Oku continued to abide by his usual duties, until, three weeks later, his father returned, an angry look in his eyes. Oku asked his father if he had acquired the knowledge of how to turn stone into water. *"No!"* replied Bulu. Shocked as to why his father was in such a foul mood, Oku asked him why he was so upset. Bulu sat the boy down and in his traditional spoken language now translated for the times said, *"Son, I was hustled."*

The story, simple and funny as it may sound, was an example of how elders could engage the young. Early stories like this were used to teach real meaningful lessons. Hustling now has a new meaning and the modern day hustler has changed from earlier ones but this was still history being passed down, and when spoken by a tribal man living in the ancient tradition, it is a true testament that even the earliest peoples knew the concept of being hustled or of being conned out of something. This story would have been used as a lesson to teach young people many different things; sometimes you might get hustled but what is important is that you tried to better yourself and you should not give up. However, the story did not end there.

Oku grew older and when he finally became old enough, he decided he would leave his village and go and find a new life elsewhere because he had a curiosity and thirst to see more. He left his village and headed into the next village, the same village his father Bulu had visited all those years before. When he arrived in this village he noticed that all the people living there were wearing around their necks the same stones the woman had shown his father. He asked why they were wearing these stones, to which one man told him of a boy in the village who had been backed into a corner by a snake. The boy had around his neck a stone and to his surprise a light from the stone shone into the snake's eyes, blinding it. So now, in this village, these stones were regarded as a token of special defence against snakes. Oku explained how his father had been hustled all those years before. Like Oku's father, others had come from all over to the village with their stones, but when they arrived and did not get any knowledge of how to turn stone into water, they just dumped their stones not wanting to carry the heavy bags home. As Oku continued to walk further

14

into the village, a bright light in the distance caught his eye. He began to walk towards it. As he got closer he saw a house built from the stones. Outside the house were women and children playing. Oku realised this house must belong to the man that hustled his father. It was a guess but he was pretty sure. The house was built of clay with diamond stones imbedded all over so that it reflected light in all directions. It looked spectacular, like nothing he had ever seen before. He entered and the man to whom the house belonged was sat there. The man asked Oku to come closer and as Oku approached him it became apparent that the man was blind. Oku told the man about his father being hustled many years before and the man explained he did not start the rumour of his ability to turn stone into water. He explained to Oku that whenever he looked at these diamond stones he could see bright colours and this gave him hope and made him feel happy so people went collecting them for him. Oku forgave the man for hustling his father and on that day he learned a lesson in value.

A true hustler must know themselves before they set out attempting to hustle. They must understand value. There are some things that are precious to one man that might not be precious to the next. Water was precious to Oku and his folk but not esteemed as highly to the blind man and his. Now rumour has it that the blind man's house fell down but the stones were buried. Thousands of years later so many children had heard this story that this became a story not about hustling, but a story about treasure.

What is important with any story or book is that someone learns a lesson. The history of hustling can go on forever but take what you have heard and use it for your own journey. One thing you have to remember is money is only as valuable as the value one gives it. It is the same for diamonds and gold. To some men even today diamonds are still just stones and gold is still just a metal.

Money is any object that is generally accepted as payment for goods, services and repayments of debts. There are different types of money. Prior to the coinage being minted at the temple of Juno other types of money existed and still do.

THE DIFFERENT TYPES OF MONEY

BARTER

This means to exchange by trade or to exchange goods or services without the use of money. For example, if a hunter had some meat and wanted to swap it with a farmer for some grain, or a friend said he would fix your broken car if you made him dinner, this is known as bartering. The aim is to try and get the best possible deal for what you want to exchange. The use of barter-like methods may date back to ancient times but people around the world still barter to this very day. There is no evidence of a society or economy that relied solely on bartering, however, one can only assume that this type of trading must have occurred as far back as man existed.

COMMODITY MONEY

Commodity money was the next important type of money developed. Commodity money is any object which is valuable in itself used to buy things, pay for services or repay debts. Examples of commodity money can be solid gold or silver coins, where the value of the metal itself far exceeds its actual given value. If an English gold sovereign has a given value of one pound sterling but its actual value in gold is very much more than one pound, this is commodity money.

Societies in the Americas, Asia, Africa and Australia used shells as commodity money, as the shell itself had a rare value to these communities. Of all the types of commodity money, gold and silver became the most popular metals to use and were traded all over the world. So you can see commodity money is far older than the coinage money of the temple of

Juno days. However, the coins and money which came from the temple of Juno developed into the type of money as you know it today, which is called fiat money.

FIAT MONEY

The word fiat means to sanction or authorize, and within the capitalist world, countries and their governments fiat their currencies as legal tender. All modern societies use fiat money. Fiat money is a typc of money where the value is not in the actual coin, banknote or object used as the money itself. When somebody has a bank note and says, *"It is just a piece of paper"*, they are not lying. The money itself has very little value. For instance, a modern pound coin used in the UK has little value in the actual metal it is made from. Instead its value is only there by government order or fiat. The government declares the fiat currency to be legal tender, making it unlawful to not accept the fiat currency as a means of repayment for all debts, public and private. As well as bank notes and coins there is bank money. Bank money is the balance held in cheque accounts and savings accounts and this usually forms by far the largest part of the money supply.

It is very important to fully grasp the concept of fiat money as this method is what the modern world uses today and this very method is what keeps the bankers in control. The banks can change the value of money. Different currencies around the world will have different values. A US dollar and a Jamaican dollar could be printed on the same piece of paper or material yet they will have completely different values. Paper money originally started as a receipt to tell you how much money you had in coins because the coins were too heavy to carry around. Before fiat money the old coins would have been made with precious metals like silver and gold, though today coins around the world are made with cheap metals. As a hustler you must study the stock market because the value of the currency you use is constantly changing.

Throughout history many wars have been fought over money; countries fighting over business deals. A president of an African country once asked the West to purchase his country's oil with gold because he did not want to be paid with fiat money. He said it was worthless to him. When he refused to take the money, war broke out and the oil was stolen. Fiat money has been used to oppress poor countries. A country may be rich in resources but if their money is worthless they will always struggle. Africa is the richest continent on the planet. Without its resources in the ground there would be no modern world because the minerals from the earth in Africa are vital for most modern technology. African countries could back their money on the resources in the ground, but this could have catastrophic effects on fiat money as the world knows it today. Cash money is slowly being digitalized so as a hustler, it is important to try and know what is coming in order to stay one step ahead. But before one deals with the future they must know more of the past.

In Africa, from approximately 5000BC, gold and other precious stones were already being traded as a form of money. Gold was used regularly in Africa and most of the earliest gold artefacts discovered in the world come from Africa. From approximately 1000 BC, small knife like shapes cast of bronze were used as money in China and the Far East. Money in the shape of coins was first manufactured in India, then China, and then in cities around the Aegean sea between 800 and 500 BC. The Aegean coins were heated hammered and stamped with a symbol. The Indian coins discovered from the Ganges river valley were punched metal disks. The Chinese coins were cast in bronze with holes in the centre of the coin so that they could be strung together for safekeeping.

Fiat currency in the form of coins first appeared at the temple of Juno in 273 BC, but fiat currency in the form of paper money or banknotes came much later in China during the Song Dynasty in 960 AD. The banknotes were named JIAOZI. Originally promise notes were used. People would promise to pay one another in coins and write this promise on a note. It came about because merchants were tired of having to carry copper coins around that could become very heavy in weight. The first banknotes in China from the Han Dynasty in 118 BC were made of leather.

Banknotes are now the most common form of fiat money and are used to pay for services and goods around the world.

HISTORY OF BANKING

History or his story of banking is part of the same story as money. Money was just seen as something valuable that could be traded, and anything that is valuable needs to be looked after safely. Whoever does the looking after of those valuables or money are loosely regarded as bankers. If the history of trade and barter dates back 100,000 years, it is likely that in the same time period there must have been transactions resembling banking going on.

A story of such is this: Reby, a small though physically strong man from the Stone Age, wants to travel to a nearby forest to collect and pick fruits and berries. However, he is afraid to leave his stash of firewood and food unattended. He goes to his friend Japes, a big strong warrior, and asks him to look after his stash whilst he is gone, promising him a cooked meal and a small sack of whatever he has foraged on his return for help. Other people approach Japes with similar propositions. Japes agrees and has a meal each time someone returns. He does not need to fight for food anymore and gets fat. Japes represents the banker. He kept people's valuables safe and received a fat profit for this.

It was the change in how people lived that stimulated a need for banking. Before 10,000BC early man would have lived with their families away from other families, somewhat like the animals they saw in the wild. Yet once the concentration of people living in one area reached higher levels, banking developed, for it would have become unsafe to leave one's possessions unattended whilst out for the day.

Grain banks or agricultural-type banks were used for hundreds of years before any type of treasure house or real banks were established. Treasure houses, where precious metals, jewels and coinage were kept, came about much later in history. These treasure houses were usually found in temples for the sole use of a city's ruler. The first rulers and kings were from Africa and they would have started the trend to collect precious stones and gold. This would have spread to other parts of the world. Later, in ancient Greece and during the Roman Empire, approximately 1,200 BC, lenders started to base themselves in temples and would give loans. This is when banking really started because it was the first time that people began to swap money and make coin deposits. Archaeology from this period in ancient China and India also shows evidence of money lending activity so banking was international even then.

The actual word bank can trace its origin back to the ancient Roman Empire where the money lenders and money changers would set up their stalls in the middle of enclosed courtyards. The stalls were long benches called '*bancu*'. Business would be conducted from here. Later in Renaissance Italy, around 1,350AD-1,500AD, the word bancu then developed into the Italian word '*banco*' meaning '*desk*' or '*bench*'. This was used by the Florentine bankers who conducted their business from these desks which were covered with green tablecloths. All transactions happened at these benches and these Italian merchants are officially known as the first real bankers in the modern sense.

Money has been used for thousands of years and will continue to be in circulation for many more years to come. Understanding its history will help you hustle with a wider knowledge of why money is used and the importance of it.

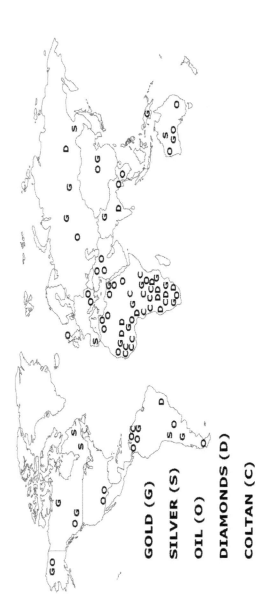

GOLD (G)

SILVER (S)

OIL (O)

DIAMONDS (D)

COLTAN (C)

CHAPTER 3

ATTRIBUTES OF A HUSTLER

Some people are naturally gifted and are able to hustle successfully because they realise that money is a necessity and making money is a form of survival. For others, hustling is not innate and must be taught. Some will have to learn from their mistakes. So do you think you have what it takes? This is a question you need to ask yourself regularly as the road to success can be a long, rocky and difficult one to tread. There are several characteristics you need to have and several that you will need to discard.

CHARACTERISTICS NEEDED TO BECOME A HUSTLER:

Motivation – *'The desire and willingness to do something'.* Without desire and the drive to succeed you cannot call yourself a hustler. Every day you should wake up full of enthusiasm, look yourself in the mirror and tell yourself, *'I am going to be rich'*. Before you eat you become hungry and this must be the same for success. Before you are to become rich you must be motivated. Positivity and confidence will help you to create and attract opportunities.

Dedication – *'To set apart and consecrate to some sacred purpose; to devote yourself to a particular cause'.* You cannot expect to achieve great success without putting in time and effort. Hard work does not guarantee success but without hard work it is impossible to achieve anything worthwhile. Do not expect hand-outs because success is not given; it is earned. No matter how many times you fail and feel the desire to give up, never quit; carry on fighting and stay in pursuit of your dreams. Quitting is for losers and this game of hustling is only for winners. The more dedicated you are to a task, the more you will appreciate the reward when it is completed.

Passion – *'An enthusiastic interest or direction of the mind'.* You need to enjoy hustling to be good at it. Many people sacrifice happiness for a pay cheque. They remain trapped in occupations they do not enjoy because they become reliant on their wages. If this is the life you choose to live, do not complain once the situation you find yourself in has drained you of all your energy and killed your spirit. Find a hustle that is enjoyable and you are passionate about. Making money should be fun.

Psychopathic tendencies – Throughout your life, situations may arise in which your personal feelings conflict with the necessities of business. Hustlers must be able to curb their emotions in such situations. The owners of large businesses fire hundreds of employees throughout their lifetime, putting their personal sentiment to one side for the sake of the company. If you conflate emotional attachment and business obligations, it may be you who finds yourself out of pocket or, worse yet, out of a job and without a hustle. That does not mean you should be cold-hearted or lacking conscience, but remember that your business should be your top priority.

Discipline – *'Training designed to engender self-control and an ordered way of life; the state of self-control achieved by such training'.* Making money takes hard work and willpower. Once you have money, being able to resist the temptation to spend money unnecessarily is not easy. As a hustler you will always be in reach of cash. You need to be able to differentiate between if you really need something or you just want it because you know you can afford it. In a later chapter you will be given some rules and guidelines that you must obey if you want to prosper. Sticking to them is up to you.

Altruism - *'Disinterested and selfless concern for the well-being of others'.* Being selfless and putting other people's interests before your own, is not only a beautiful way to be, but it is the fastest route to success. There is a saying, 'What you give, you get back.' A better saying is, 'What you give you get back tenfold.' This is because positive energy attracts more positive energy. Two stars shine brighter than one. If you are able to help others the universe will help you. Your kindness will be rewarded.

CHARACTERISTICS TO DISCARD:

Laziness – *'Reluctant to exert oneself; averse to work; sluggish'.* If you are unwilling to put hard work and energy into your hustling then thinking you will become rich is delusional. You need to be organised, punctual and reliable. Even if you are jobless and have no plans you should still wake up early with the intent of making money every day. Your new positive attitude will begin to bring you all sorts of opportunities.

Greed – *'An eager desire or longing for more than one's share'.* Thinking you need to be greedy to become rich is a myth. Selfishness damages your reputation. No one wants to do business with someone who is only concerned with his or her own profit. True hustlers not only want themselves to become rich but they want everyone around them to live the good life. Greediness might make money in the short-term but nobody will work with you again once they have discovered your true colours so you will lose out in the long run. Giving to the less fortunate will help you to feel better about what you are doing and even give you a purpose. Other people you work with can be greedy too, so be aware of this. If any profit goes missing, for example, it may well be a greedy partner; a corrupt hustler.

Negativity – *'The expression of criticism of or pessimism about something'.* If you doubt your own and other's capabilities you are lost before you have even started. Pessimism releases negative energy which will act as a deterrent to others around you.

Ignorance – *'Lack of information or knowledge'.* Ignorant people are not popular and if ignorant you can come across as rude or impolite. You may believe you are knowledgeable in subjects that you actually lack an understanding of. Being illiterate and uneducated means you have no real basis for opinions and arguments so always be open to learning new things, as nobody knows everything.

Arrogance – *'Having or revealing and exaggerated sense of one's own importance or abilities'.* You will never prosper as a hustler if you think you are better than others. It is okay to take pride in what you do and being confident can be a good thing but there is a limit, a line that you can cross where your arrogance augments into an inflated sense of superiority. This is a characteristic that needs to be discarded. Do not try to exaggerate your importance or abilities. Never forget where you came from. If you think you are better than other hustlers then your egotism will bring only hatred and jealousy and you will lose the love and respect you once had.

Fear – *'Afraid of danger'.* Most people are scared of losing money so they do not invest in anything. It is good to be cautious with your money but you must be able to determine if your fear is stopping you from making money.

Hustling can be compared to a game in which not every player can win. Winning equals success, and success equals money. Every individual will approach the game in their own way but these characteristics are vital if you want to accomplish your goal.

CHAPTER 4

KNOWLEDGE

You might have heard that '*money is power*'. The real truth, however, is that '*knowledge is power*' because money does not make you rich; it is knowing what to do with it that does. If you want to become a hustler, you must increase your knowledge of money, how to make money and what to do with it once you have it.

Enlighten yourself to the true power of knowledge because without it you are just a slave, a pawn, a peasant to governments and rulers. People who are highly educated always rule the ignorant and unfortunately the world you have been born into has already been moulded so that certain families and the more privileged class will obtain positions of power through conditioning and unfair circumstances. Take an army general who controls thousands of troops: he might not be as strong, quick or agile as his foot soldiers; his dexterity in handling weapons might be second-rate when compared to his rifle men, yet his superior knowledge grants him power and jurisdiction over those of lesser intelligence.

Knowledge is a very important thing in life. Learning and striving to understand new things, gives you the ability to create a sense of freedom. Educating yourself as much as possible in a wide range of subjects and fields will lessen your need to rely on others, because you yourself will be able to solve the problems you are faced with. Material objects, including money, can be lost at any given time. Knowledge, on the other hand, once attained, cannot be lost, and the opportunities afforded to you will encourage you to continue furthering your education. You might learn of a method to make money quickly without much effort. Then one day something happens that causes you to lose that money, yet because you have learned how to make money in this particular way, the method can simply be implemented again so you are hardly out of pocket.

Knowledge can also be misused and become dangerous. You may wonder how understanding of a certain subject can endanger yourself and others, or why someone would use what they know destructively. Knowledgeable men created the engine, and with it enabled transportation through locomotives and automobiles. However, with this same knowledge, man helped facilitate the production of military vehicles used against one another for destructive means. Many of the world's diseases were created by scientists in laboratories, and most have a cure, but curing disease is not always the most profitable avenue to take. Treating disease generates more profit than curative measures, and so patients are often kept sick and in constant need of expensive medicine to prop up their lives, but not to be in an optimum state of health. Understanding all of this provides you with a different perspective on life and allows you to appreciate how evil knowledge can be if harnessed for destructive or unethical means. Just because you can does not mean that you should.

And do not believe everything you read, see, or hear. The news stories broadcast on television stations are not necessarily true stories but stories that those in charge want the public to see and hear; the story that sells the newspapers, the story that will manipulate the people to think in a certain way. These stories are exaggerated and distorted to influence the public to believe what those in power intend for their subjects to believe. Not only should you be mindful of the media but also of history books. Remember history is just *'his story'* and his story may be a lie. Nations are biased and may write and rewrite history in ways that generate hatred towards other nations and peoples it either dislikes or has disputes with. You must learn to carry out your own research so that you can distinguish the lies from the truth. There are two sides to every coin and two sides to every story. You must hear both sides of a situation to make your own judgements and separate facts from fiction. Examining as many different sources of information as possible will bring you closer to the truth.

Read as many books about money as possible, study accounting, investing, the economy and what is happening in the financial world. Everything that is happening and has happened affects you so why not find out how and why? Children are hardly taught anything about finance in schools and the education schools provide is not a guarantee that their students will become rich or successful. Children can learn from their parents and older siblings about money, but if these individuals have not become successful, what can they really learn from them? Adults need to learn how to become hustlers so they can impart this knowledge to the young.

You need to learn about money to be able to make it as a hustler. You cannot expect to become rich overnight; you must study and work hard. Most people learn how to hustle from just trying to make some extra cash. They learn from the streets, from the environment and from the people they are surrounded by, but if they are living in a deprived area and the people they socialize with are poor, how will they ever prosper? The truth is that they will not; that is not until they decide to do something about it themselves. How many times have you heard older people say, *'If only I could be young again with the knowledge I have now, I would be rich!'* Learn to hustle from an early age so that you do not make the mistakes most adults regret. And if you are older, remember it is never too late to find success so do not give up before you have found it. If you are interacting with the young teach them what you know. Everyone can be a hustler; everyone can be rich.

The majority of people are not educated about money and when faced with a monetary problem they find challenging, they usually give up. They will ask for advice from other people and in doing this will never learn how to solve their own problems. The rich are rich because they face challenges head on. By solving your problems yourself, you will learn more, especially if you make mistakes, because you will learn not to make them again. The knowledge you learn should be shared with the people around you because you never know when you might need to rely on them.

A good way to learn about money making is to speak to and take advice from the rich and successful who are actually hustlers in the true sense. Pay heed to advice from someone who is experienced in the subject you are asking about. Do not approach a footballer about property, go to a property developer; do not contact an architect about book keeping, go to an accountant. You too should become the best at what you do because eventually you will be paid for it. Nevertheless, sometimes it is not wise to focus only on one subject your whole life. For example, you might spend years training and working as a builder and then sustain an injury. How will you find another job if you only know one trade and have no other skills? These are all things to think about.

The rich use money to make more money. If you do not understand how to invest, how can you really get rich? Getting good grades in school, college or university does not guarantee that you are going to make money. Some of the most successful people in the world have no qualifications. However, it is vital to learn the basics of some subjects: English, maths, science and IT can all assist you on your journey to success. Learning different languages can also offer advantages because as a hustler you may be doing deals with people from all over the world.

English is the most used language in the world so it helps to understand the basics. As a hustler you need to communicate, read and write properly. Mastering your maths skills will help you make money for money making involves numbers. You should at least know the basics of adding, subtracting, multiplication and division. Being good at maths will also help you to do your own bookkeeping and keep financial records to avoid an employee skimming any money from you. Keeping your own records will also inform you of precisely how much money you are making or losing.

Understanding nature and the planet man inhabits means one must have a deeper understanding also of the sciences. Maths and English can only take you so far but without understanding science you cannot achieve greatness.

In this ever-changing world computers are becoming more and more important. Technology will continue to improve and so knowing how to use a computer is a necessity.

Once you have left school and finished your studies it is easy to forget skills and knowledge you have learned. Once in a while it will benefit you to do a recap course to refresh your mind. Doing different types of brainteasers and puzzles will also help to keep the brain exercised. The

brain is a muscle and like the muscles one develops from years of gym workouts, the brain suffers without regular exercise. If you do not continue to train and push yourself mentally you will forget what you have learned. You will find yourself struggling with simple things you would have previously found easy. Knowledge is freedom.

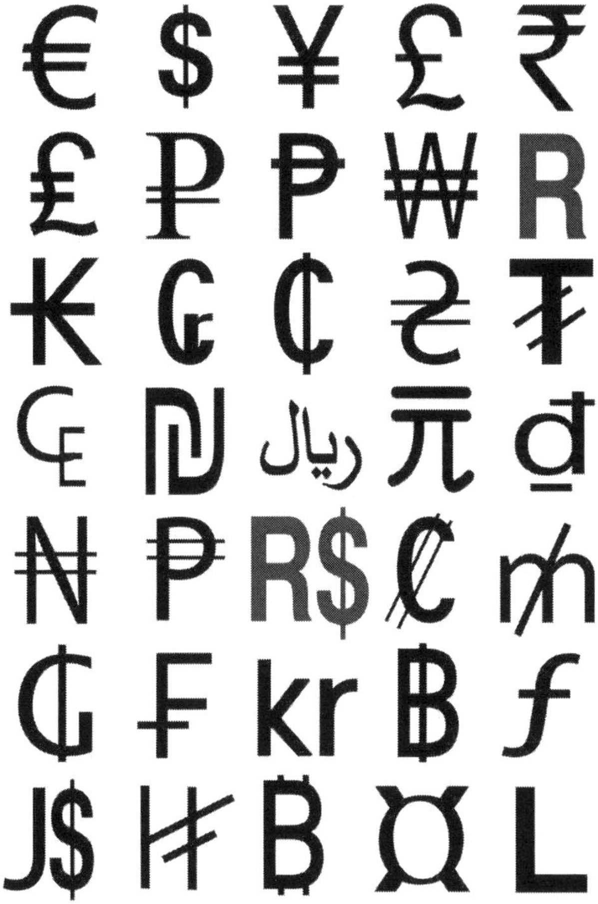

CHAPTER 5

IMAGE

The way you dress and carry yourself can have a major impact on how successful you are as a hustler. If you do not already have a good reputation or successful formula for making money then potential clients, customers and business partners will judge you on the way you dress and behave.

The world has become much too concerned with the way people look. Though originating in the West, materialistic attitudes have spread to the East and, even in some of the most remote and poverty stricken countries, people are now worried about their appearances. Human beings judge one another. They make assumptions about the people they see and meet during their lives. Therefore, if you want to become a true hustler, dressing and behaving like one is important. Hustlers work for themselves; it is both a way of life and an occupation. You are your own boss and this requires appropriate attire. In all workplaces there are codes of conduct, ways to behave and dress. You have to consider this every day you are hustling. People want to do business with those who are positive and enthusiastic. They want to work with a man or woman who looks as if they are living well; it gives the impression that these individuals know what they are doing and if you were to work with such a person then maybe you could achieve the same. But before you go out and spend money on a nice wardrobe make sure you know how to conduct yourself because people will see through the image if you do not. Do not let the new attention go to your head; just because you look the part does not mean that you are... yet.

Take into consideration your audience. If you are attending a formal business meeting you should wear a suit; if you are meeting with fellow street hustlers you might wear some of the latest designer labels, something eye-catching. There is a reason for tailoring what you are wearing to a specific audience; you want to leave a lasting impression upon those you are interacting with, making the message you are communicating as influential and effective as can be.

DRESS CODE

♦ Try wearing a suit for a day and notice the new attention you will receive.

♦ Fresh, clean shoes show you take pride in your appearance. They are normally one of the first things someone looks at after meeting and greeting.

♦ A sharp, clean haircut shows you are well groomed, which is a sign of wealth.

♦ A good watch promotes success and adds the finishing touch to the whole image.

♦ Hoods attract the wrong kind of attention. They are associated with crime and people who are wrongdoing. These stereotypes might not be necessarily true. For example, there are many designer clothes with hoods that legit people wear. However, stereotypical appearances of a criminal negates that you should not be wearing one, especially if you are hustling on the wrong side of the law.

♦ Tracksuits are made for sports and going to the gym; do not wear tracksuits to do business. They might be comfortable but they propagate the wrong image if you want to look successful.

♦ Remember, dressing down can be appropriate too, if you feel too much in the spotlight, do not wish to draw attention to yourself, or simply want to mind your own business rather than reveal it to others.

Some very important scientific information that is never taught is the significance of colours. It is one of the most valuable things to remember when it comes to appearance and image when doing business. Different colours evoke different moods. Successful businessmen will have some understanding of this but only the super-rich will understand it on a deeper level. Many of them employ stylists who dress them in particular colours and designs for prominent events.

Colours have always interested spiritual people. Around the world different civilizations will view colours slightly differently to one another. However, there are some key techniques in understanding colours and the relation they play with business.

Some things you should consider before doing business are as follows: decide what state you are in. Are you feeling good? Do you have a lot of energy? Are you nervous? Once you know the state of your being you can use colours to aid you; not just by the colours you wear but even down to the colour of the room you are planning to conduct your business deals in. Research the background of those you are doing business with. What colours will change their mood? What may put them on guard or what might relax them? To win a game of chess you need to be moves ahead of your opponent and to be successful in business you must also be moves ahead.

COLOURS

Black - This colour is the greatest colour of all as it absorbs all other colours. In business black shows strength and power. A black suit will look more powerful than a grey or blue one. Black is also a colour that has been feared throughout the ages. Black has been associated with people of African origin and people with darker skin. If one labels a person black they will unconsciously fear that person without even realising it, so it is important not to label humans with colours.

Purple - This colour is close to black but has a reddish tone. It is a passionate colour. Often purple is associated with the senses. If one is doing business with the opposite sex they may wish to use purple to seduce that person to feel more and think less.

Red - This colour could be viewed as the most important colour to be aware of. It can signify many different things and this can be tricky when doing business. Red has always been associated with danger but danger does not always stand for something bad. Blood is red and can represent harm or death but blood is also life. Red is the colour of making a stance; a statement. Like purple, it is a passionate colour. In China and the Far East red is a lucky colour.

Brown - This colour is an earthly colour. It is the colour of the tree's bark and the soil in the ground. It represents life much more than the colour red. It gives life. This colour will calm people down when doing business. If you feel nervous, a brown piece of clothing or brown surroundings could help you to keep yourself composed.

Green - This colour is the colour of nature; nature's very own colour. A perfect example of when to use this colour would be while conducting business with a person who is very stubborn or with someone who is selfish. Green clothing or doing business outside in natural surroundings could help to open up people or associates and make them come round to where you want them to be.

Blue - This is the colour of water. Water flows. Water can be hot or cold. Using science in business can be a simple thing like giving a person a hot drink on a cold day; and the colour blue, which represents cold, can be good at counteracting the colour red, which represents hot. If the people you are doing business with are oppositional and wearing lots of red, then wear blue to make them see your strength; to make them back down. However, keep in mind that opposing colours do not always make for good business.

Orange - This is the colour of the sunset and the sunrise. The sun is strongly associated with God. The sun gives life to everything on the planet. The colour orange is the colour of leadership. The boss of a company or small business should wear orange often to assert his or her authority.

Gold - This colour, so often the colour of jewellery, is associated with wealth. However, it will also attract the evil eye. If you wish to show off wealth, you must be willing to accept the negative energy it will bring with it. Gold is a very powerful colour, not one to be taken lightly.

Yellow - This is the colour of fire. Fire brings warmth and heat. Warmth and heat is a sign of friendship. Wearing the colour yellow will evoke friendship and trust when conducting business.

White - This colour is the lightest of all the colours. Nothing alive in nature is pure white and so traditionally it has been associated with ghosts or the supernatural. Like black, it is not good to associate this colour to people. There are no white people on this planet. When doing business, the colour white is good for first encounters. It has few connotations, allowing one to build a relationship immediately without any preconceptions. It is a neutral colour and acts like a blank slate.

There is more to appearances than meets the eye so remember to be cautious. Research shows that people judge and make assumptions about others based on their appearance within seven seconds of meeting them. With this in mind, be aware that first impressions are very important in hustling.

CHAPTER 6

COMMUNICATION

Communication is the act of transferring information from one place to another. How well this information is transferred is a measure of how good your communication skills are. The way you talk to people can take you a long way in the hustling world. You need to master this skill because without it you will struggle to progress as a hustler. Clear, effective communication and positive energy are essential.

A hustler needs to be able to speak with a variety of different people, altering their tone or slant to suit the audience. Try speaking in a manner that is comfortable and familiar to the person you are speaking with. If you are in the East End of London speaking with a cockney, you might want to incorporate a little more slang into your speech. If you are conversing with someone whose background is more upper class then you might need to keep in check any informal language. If you are not self-confident you must develop your interpersonal skills and become more assertive, as you will need to be decisive and self-assured to perfectly hustle. Being assertive means standing up for what you believe in and expressing yourself honestly and comfortably. Whilst asserting yourself it is important to look out for your best interests but it is just as important to consider other's feelings. Remember you have two ears and one mouth so you should always listen more than you talk. A key component of communication is the ability to listen well. This is vital to understanding exactly what the message being communicated to you is.

NETWORKING

'It is not what you know but who you know.' Without connections you will never be able to hustle correctly. You cannot judge a book by its cover and the same goes for a hustler. Always approach others and ask what it is they do. Build relationships with a variety of people from all different backgrounds; someone could prove useful to you and your business. Not only does networking put you in contact with people who can help you and your business, but it also allows you to discover clients and customers. You have to ask to know if someone wants to buy your product or use your service. Keeping track of buyers and sellers makes

networking one of the most important things to do as a hustler. Building relationships with business partners, clients and customers is the key to effective networking. You want to leave a lasting impression on your new clientele, so find things you share in common to discuss with them, and try not to talk strictly about business. Share jokes, have a laugh, and always stay real. Remain professional and polite at all times and show your potential client or business partner a high degree of respect. You need to communicate what it is you do in a short matter of time, exhibiting why your client needs you and why you need them. Do not force your pitch, as this could seem unprofessional and off-putting. You do not want to make potential clients or business partners nervous or uncomfortable. Make sure to exchange contact details. If you are given a business card, store the number into your mobile device or phonebook as they can be easy to misplace.

CODE TALK

Code talk dates back to ancient times. People have often disguised language to keep outsiders from knowing what they are talking about. Many styles of language came about in this very way. Common slang already exists and new words and terminology are constantly emerging. If everyone on the streets becomes familiar with such terminology it is likely the authorities have caught on too. As a street hustler staying on point is a must. There will be people who should not know your business; and you can never be sure of who is listening in to your conversations. Devise and develop your own code talk to use within your circle. Do not let anyone but your circle know your code. This will ensure that you are always talking with some degree of privacy and will keep your business safe. Fake names are a great way to avoid detection, but remember to keep them realistic. An unrealistic name in the presence of others could alert them of a suspicious conversation. As well as code talk, it is smart to develop code signals, hand gestures and body movements that only you and your friends understand the meaning to. Do not make them too obvious, as this will be noticed. Keep the movements and signals discreet.

Code talk is used at all levels of business, not just in the street. Commercial, district high-flyers and corporate elites use code all the time. For example, a businessman presenting a new idea to potential investors might have some colleagues present during a meeting. If he forgets to mention a particular aspect of his idea or says something wrong, then his colleagues can use a code signal or code talk to make him remember or become aware of mistakes. This would allow the hustler to rectify all errors and impress potential investors without them noticing anything has gone wrong.

PHONES AND MOBILE DEVICES

Phones and mobile devices are an essential tool for any hustler. A good hustler should always have credit or minutes to talk on their phone because communication is the main part of any deal or transaction.

Phones are not always safe to talk on, especially as tracking technology such as GPRS continues to develop. If you are found to be in the area of a crime, GPRS evidence can be used against you. Phone calls can be monitored too so talking in codes and switching numbers is what the best hustlers do, to stay ahead of the authorities and anyone else who may pose a threat. Be aware that the authorities can remotely activate the microphone in your mobile phone to listen to your conversation from a distance. It is not uncommon for criminal hustlers to leave their numbers unregistered and to make purchases without the use of a credit card, so that nothing can be linked back to them.

EMAIL

Before the invention of the internet there was no email. Mail was sent by post. This practice still goes on but as the world develops and changes technology is taking over. Email is now one of the most commonly used forms of communication. Like talking on a phone, everything said in email is recorded. This form of communication always leaves a trail so watch what you write.

Always be clear when conversing with a fellow hustler to avoid any later disappointments or misunderstandings. There are two types of communication: one-way communication is when you share information with customers, clients and other hustlers but do not accept any responses - advertising and promoting are examples; two-way communication is when the customer, client or fellow hustler is able to respond. This can be helpful as you can receive feedback and advice for future business.

Furthermore, there are three primary ways to communicate. These are through verbal communication, written communication or expressive communication (body language). It is wise to use a combination of all three when hustling as people process information in different ways. Some people need to hear information to get the point; others might need to see information written down to fully comprehend what you are communicating to them. When communicating with someone in person it is important to keep in mind the power of perception. You might want to get a certain message across but the way a person perceives it, or interprets it, might be different to what you intended, so take perception very seriously.

Communication skills must be developed to improve the outcome of every interaction you have. Ask questions to ensure you have correctly interpreted the message any speaker is delivering; and remember that listening is part of communication too. When delivering your own message you must be sure to plan and clarify in your head what you are trying to convey. Listen to feedback and not to your own thoughts to make sure your listener or audience understands perfectly what it is you are trying to say; all the points you are trying to make.

CHAPTER 7

SAVING

Nobody knows what tomorrow will bring. There is no telling when a problem that could affect you financially will arise. Saving money, especially if you are able to make interest on your savings, will help safeguard your finances and prepare you for any difficulties that might come your way.

A financial advisor would tell you that you should try to save something like 10% of your earnings for the future. As a hustler, you should aim to save 50%. This might seem like a lot initially, but if you do not save a large portion of your earnings, you could end up wasting what you have worked hard for. The biggest problem people face when they have money is the urge to spend it when they see something that they want but do not necessarily need. If you keep your money readily accessible then this temptation will be even greater. You must learn to control your desire to spend if you want to save money.

Saving money does not necessarily mean you have to put your earnings in a bank; it could be invested in assets. Long-term investments are also a good way of saving money too. Some investments will require you to tie your money up for a number of years, and so prevent you from dipping into these savings, no matter how drawn you are to spending sprees. You will receive interest on the money you invest at the end of the time period decided upon by you and your investor. Keep in mind that if you decide to take your money early, you might be breaking your contract and could be fined.

Hustlers on both sides of the law need to save. However, any money made in an illegal fashion must be laundered before it is saved. Laundering money allows you to explain where your money came from if you are ever asked by the authorities. When saving money decide why you are saving money. Are you saving to buy something or to start something; or are you planning to leave money to someone or a number of people?

When saving money you must understand the differences between assets, liabilities and expenses as they will affect you on a daily basis.

ASSETS

There are many different types of assets. Assets can be cash, bonds, shares, property, patents, objects of art and so on. In essence, an asset is anything that brings you an income. Some say an asset is also something that has a resale value, but if it costs you more money to maintain it, is it an asset or a liability? The rich and wealthy invest always in assets, and with the profit they make they buy more assets. They enact a constant cycle, whereby a purchased asset earns enough income to purchase another, then another, until enough assets are owned and providing a large enough income so that they become financially free.

LIABILITIES

A liability is something that costs money to keep. An everyday car, for example, can be a liability as it costs money to run and fix. Liabilities should be disposed of; or better still they should be turned into assets. A car can be turned into an asset in the sense that your use of it will earn you more money than you would stand to lose without it. The more liabilities you can turn into assets, the better.

EXPENSES

Something that you have to spend money on is an expense. Money spent on carrying out a job or task will be an expense. Expenses are often unavoidable, but should be minimised as much as possible.

EXAMPLES

ASSETS	LIABILITIES	EXPENSES
Property owned outright	Property with mortgage	Utilities
		Food
Stocks and shares	Cars	Taxes
	Pets	Taking care of family
Royalties		

Remember circumstances can always change and assets can become liabilities; liabilities can become assets, assets can become expenses and expenses can become assets. In order for something to be a true asset that asset must be fully paid for. If it is not, it may become a liability or an expense. For example, a property bought with a mortgage is not an asset until it is yours. If you miss a few payments to the mortgage lender it will quickly become repossessed and taken from you. Therefore a property with a mortgage must go into the liability section.

The rich continue to get richer because they understand that the aim is to try to increase their income and assets while decreasing their expenses and liabilities.

Try to find a way of saving money that suits you. There was a well-known shotta who dealt with surplus amounts of cash on a daily basis. At this time, the new £20 note had recently been introduced so he decided to save every one of these notes he came by. Before he knew it, his savings were into the thousands. As a cash-handling hustler this is a good way of saving money. There are many different ways to stack money. Try to find your own method and make sure you stick to it. Before you know it you will be sitting on a big stack. A lot of people think they are rich because they have money in the bank but if you do not continue to earn an income your money will start to decrease because of the cost of living.

Remember the more business you can bring to a company or person, the cheaper you may get what you are buying, saving you money. For example, if a shotta is told a kilo of cannabis is going to cost £6,000 but he gathers together a few other shottas who all want a kilo as well, his connect might give him a better deal, as in four kilos for £20,000. So by picking up together he just got his kilo for £5,000, saving himself £1,000 off the original price.

You need to have a target. How will you ever be satisfied with your financial situation if you do not? When you get on a train you have a final stop to get off at. This destination is similar to your target. You have to plan your journey or route of how you are going to get there. How long will it take? Is there a shortcut; or would you prefer to stay on the same steady journey even though you know it is going to take a longer time? And the most important thing to think about is what are you going to do when you reach your destination?

CHAPTER 8

BUYING AND SELLING

People who do not work and grind for their money spend it without thinking because they do not appreciate the real value of it. Doing this leaves them with no savings. On the other hand, tight people are scared to spend their money and do not get to enjoy what they have worked so hard for. It is best to try to find a balance.

Try not to buy what you cannot afford. Do not loan or borrow money just to purchase something you have set your eyes on. Work hard and eventually you can buy it with your own money without paying any interest to a lender. Ask a lot of questions when you buy something. You do not need to rush. Make sure you do research first. You can always find a better price for something if you look hard enough. Make sure you are getting good value for money. Sometimes it is good to look at all of your possessions and see what was really worth the price you paid. Try to identify what you are wasting money on. If you do this every month eventually you will be able to get rid of your bad spending habits.

Spending money is often a source of pride for many people, but a true hustler will swallow theirs if it means saving money. *'No-one ever choked to death from swallowing their pride.'* There was once a boy who went to prison. Whilst he was there the prison provided him and any other prisoner who asked, with free toothpaste and soap. All of the prisoners were too proud to use the prison issued toiletries and so they spent their money on different brands, but the boy, on the other hand, refused to spend money on things he could get from the authorities for free. When they were released, the other prisoners had little left in their accounts; the boy had over £3,000. Everyone has to keep a little pride in life but it should never affect any money making ventures.

When it comes to buying clothes, your pride can make you spend more as most people are materialistic in this day and age. They will wear branded items even if it costs them a small fortune. You will never catch a real hustler wearing anything that is fake or cheap, however, the hustler has weighed up the situation carefully. They know that by dressing well they are likely to attract positive attention so they will incur no losses. You have to decide if a brand or label is adding unnecessary costs; whether the branded clothes are absolute essentials.

If not purchasing a brand or label, you have to weigh up whether you are getting value for money. Take two t-shirts: one is designer, the other is unknown, but they look similar at a glance. The designer one costs £50; the unknown one costs £10. Are you paying £40 more for a label or is the quality better? Will you get more positive attention from a potential client so that the extra £40 might be worth it? The cheaper version might be so bad that it falls apart in a month. The designer one might last a whole year; so in actual fact, it is costing you less than half of what the unknown brand would cost over a year.

Everyday brands verses labels will trouble you when making decisions about what to buy. Be sensible. Research any brands and companies you are drawn to. Would you feel comfortable giving your money to a company if you knew the chairman was a pedophile or racist? Decide who you want to do business with. Those who are successful and affluent take time when spending money; they make sure they spend it with people they know having used them time after time. This way the money is retained by the same businesses helping them to become rich. Many communities have flourished using this idea.

Be aware that when you purchase something, most of the time you will have to continue spending your money on this item to maintain its use. When you buy a car you have to pay for petrol and maintenance. When you buy a mobile phone you have to pay for calling credit. If you are inventing a product, true hustlers will keep this in mind. The key is to design something that will keep the buyer coming back to you to spend more money. Therefore, the customer becomes a lifetime customer, rather than paying for a one-off service. Mobile phone companies design their technology in such a way that you can only buy applications for that device from the same company. When you buy a company specific car, only that company sells the parts you need when the old one breaks. The true hustling money makers make sure when you return to buy what is needed, it is only they who can provide for you.

NEGOTIATING

You need to know how to negotiate. This is another important skill in hustling. You cannot be shy when it comes to this; confidence is everything. Most things in life are priced above their real value and what the seller is willing to accept. You must always ask for a cheaper price no matter what. This way you will get closer to finding out the true value. A little trick is to tell the seller you can get what you are buying cheaper elsewhere from a rival seller, and do your research because you usually can. Watch out because sellers have all sorts of tactics to convince you to buy from them. One they often employ is, *'buy-now for a discount'*, telling you that the discount will not be around next week. In reality, if the seller can knock down the prices today, they can do it next week too. Do not fall for the tricks or tactics. Furniture chains use this method all the time; they advertise a discount sale as if it is just about to finish, when in reality the sale goes on all year round.

When shopping, often when you look at a price tag there is a bigger price crossed out with a new smaller price. Usually the smaller price was the original selling price; they just wrote the bigger one to make you feel like you are getting a bargain. Jewellery shops are experts in tactical sales. They always overprice their items, sometimes by hundreds, thousands or even millions of pounds. They do this because rich buyers or stupid ones are so arrogant, naive and ignorant they refuse to ask for a lower price because of some sort of loss of pride. Always haggle with them. Remember a retailer would rather you buy something with a tiny profit from them than to buy nothing at all. The way you ask can be a factor in the haggling process. If you demand something you usually will not get it cheaper, but if you ask in a friendly way you might. Set a target you are willing to pay and if you do not get it be ready to walk away. A seller's reputation is important to them so by telling them you will become a regular customer, saying good things about them and sending them other buyers, you might get a discount because they believe they will get future sales. Consider all the tricks and tactics when you are the seller too. In this way you will be aware of what clients and customers are up to. Never let yourself be duped.

BUYING A CAR

Do not HP (higher purchase) a car unless you find a 0% finance rate, which is rare and almost unheard of now. If you do find a company who offers this then maybe it should be considered. When you HP a car you end up paying double, sometimes triple what the car is worth. Swallow your pride and buy a car you can really afford; one that suits your needs not necessarily your image. With new cars, remember, as soon as you drive out of the showroom, your new car has just lost thousands of pounds in value. Why? Because, now, nobody can purchase it new; it is now a second-hand car. It does not matter what the mileage is or what the condition of the paintwork is like, it will just never be brand new again. Always carry out an official check on the background of the car. Whatever part of the world you are in, if there is no official check that can take place, take a mechanic with you to check the car over. A car might not be what it appears to be. It could have been stolen, recovered or crashed and repaired. The mileage might not be genuine. Make sure if you are buying a car privately to view it in daylight so you can check for any damage or things you would not see in the dark. More often than not, cars are not an asset. If something continues to lose value and does not earn you an income, it is a liability because it costs money to run and maintain it. As a hustler without a car, you would not be able to get around in the speed and style you do, which helps you to continue making money, so having a car is something you have to weigh up carefully.

BUYING A HOUSE

Do not rent a house. Technically you are just paying to borrow the house while you live there. A real hustler will find a way to get a deposit and a mortgage for the house because after you have done that the payments you make on your mortgage would be the same if not less than the rental fee, but only now you will own the house once you have paid off the mortgage. If you do a lot of homework you could find a bargain depending on how good the market is at the time of buying. Make sure to research all the different mortgage deals you are offered if you cannot buy the house outright. Use a solicitor that has been recommended or has a good reputation for securing deals fast as some may move too slow which can affect your pocket. Consider how quick the seller wants to move as this can also affect you directly. Will you need temporary accommodation? Will the other party wanting to relocate fast increase your chances of getting a discounted price? Always be available while the buying is in process as you might want to raise queries or other parties might have questions too.

This will be one of the most important purchases in your life so there is a lot to think about. Look at the market and find out if it is a good time to buy. Do not be desperate to be a house owner; make sure your finances are in check first. For a decent rate on your mortgage you will need a bigger deposit so maybe waiting until you can really afford such an amount is the right thing to do. Keep in mind that once you have purchased your house there may be additional fees to put it in order, so be ready for them. Location is everything. If you have the option of buying land and building your house to your own design, you get exactly what you want and you can save a lot of money in the long run.

Here are some of the costs involved in purchasing a house:

♦ Legal fees

♦ Mortgage arrangement fee

♦ Valuation fee

♦ Stamp duty

♦ Surveys

♦ Removal costs

♦ Repairs, refurbishments and decorations

Completing a deal takes time so have patience. Different countries will have different practices and legal procedures so do your research if buying in a country you are not familiar with. You search and find the property you desire; you place an offer, wait for acceptance, survey the property, pay a deposit and finally complete the deal once both parties are happy to sign. Compare the market to be sure you get your value for money.

Questions you need to ask before you buy:

♦ How long has the house been on the market?

♦ How many offers have been made?

♦ Will the property increase in value?

♦ What renovations has the house had?

♦ Has the house had any subsidence?

♦ What council tax band is the house in?

♦ What fittings and fixtures are included?

♦ If not a freehold property, how long is the lease?

♦ Is there parking?

♦ Who are the neighbours?

♦ Are there good local shops and schools?

♦ What is the transport like?

There are other questions but these are the most important. It is a good idea to write a list before you go to view or make an offer and be sure to ask all of them to the owner or selling agent. Check over the whole house, every single detail so that you do not discover problems in the future when it is too late to do anything about them. Are you planning on staying in the house until you die or are you hoping to make a profit if you resell it? Consider whether you can get a private deal and avoid all the middleman costs. Some buyers get lucky and find a seller before a house is even put on the market. A good tactic is to write a letter and post copies to all the houses you have your eye on. You never know; you might get the reply you were hoping for.

In this hustling game you will see money go to a lot of people's heads. Laziness can set in and there are some individuals who think they are a boss before they even own a business just because they have some money to their name. This is ego. To be a truly successful hustler you must have your ego under control. Simple things, you should do for yourself, instead of paying someone else to do them for you. Do not try to be a boss before you have an idea of what it is like to be a worker. Have an understanding of the lower levels of your business.

It is fine to pay others if there is some risk involved you do not wish to take yourself, however, make your employees aware of any risk. You can pay someone to take the heat or if the task involved is too time consuming and you know you could be elsewhere making more money. But if it is something petty like going to a shop or picking up a delivery, then why pay someone when you could do it yourself? If it costs £100 to pay a worker to collect some stock that will take an hour to pick up, maybe it is worth it if you are guaranteed to make more than a £100 in that same hour doing something else. Consider carefully if something you can do yourself will save you money or lose you money before you make your decision to complete a job.

Just because you have a good product does not mean you can sell it well. Someone with a poorer product might be able to move it on quickly and make more money in the process. A shotta might have better quality food than another but because he has a dead line he hardly sells. The other shotta fares better with poor quality food but a busy line. How many times have you heard about the gifted artist who is making pennies and the untalented artist who is making millions? Knowing how to sell yourself is essential. Just because you have a gift or talent does not mean you will get paid for it.

Sometimes you have to assume a role before it becomes reality. By dressing, behaving and acting as a wealthy person, people will want to work with you rather than the man or woman who looks as if they are struggling to get by. Money attracts money. You will notice the more money you make, the more people will bring you money making opportunities. Sell people an illusion of wealth and before you know it, more

hustling opportunities will present themselves to you.

CHAPTER 9

BUDGETING

When making money you need to learn how to budget in order to maximize your profits. Do not confuse your desires and luxuries with your necessities; the things you really cannot do without. Wanting something is different to needing something.

If you are trying to budget, giving yourself pocket money can help. Give yourself a weekly amount you can spend, so as to prevent you from dipping into your savings. Every hustler has their own method which works for them. A good method many use is separating money into different pockets. Hustlers usually have a stash of money they carry around with them. Any cash you are intending to save or invest goes into your left pocket and change you can spend freely goes into the right.

The less money you have the more you need to budget, and the more you budget, the more money you will save. Writing lists of your weekly expenses can help. Write down everything you spend money on, then prioritise what is most important. An electricity bill is higher priority than a ticket to a football match because you need electricity to function at home. Going to watch a game is a luxury. Try to cut down on unnecessary spending and find cheaper alternatives to things you purchase regularly.

STARTING A FAMILY

Starting a family is usually a lifelong expense but part of the cycle of life. As a hustler you must not look at family life as a burden but as a blessing. If it means you have to work twice as hard or put in triple effort then so be it. Having children will mean you need to grind harder and increase your income. After adultery and infidelity it has been researched and proven that financial problems are the biggest cause of why most relationships fall apart. Try comparing the family life of humans to the lion's kingdom. The female lions go out to hunt for meat to bring back to feed the cubs. The male lions protect the pride and regulate everything. The female lions will also teach the cubs how to hunt and kill, passing on these skills and knowledge for survival. When people have children they need to do the same. Humans need to teach their offspring how to survive in the jungle or wilderness that is this harsh world.

The harsh reality is if you cannot hunt for a job and successfully find one to get the meat, the dough, you will not be able to provide for your family.

Family life differs around the world. Different societies have different family cultures; their priorities are not the same. However, the bare necessities of any family, no matter where they are from, are food and shelter. As a hustler it is important to teach your family about money because you do not want to work hard only to see the fruits of your labour go to waste because no one is aware of how they came about; of how hard you have worked to accumulate your wealth. It is essential, if you wish the people you love to prosper along with you. The more dependant families are on outsiders the more expenses they will have. Learning basic skills from one another will keep costs down. If families grew their own food and traded within their communities they could save a fortune. Giving different family members roles within the household will help save time; and time is money.

Since families have their own structures, everyone has to adapt to their own situation. Single parents raising children by themselves might find life harder than families with two parents. The single parent might have to budget more because money has to last longer. Some children have no parents or any other relatives; they will have to learn from their surroundings and seek knowledge from elders and mentors. Whatever your situation is, you must embrace it and give life everything you have got. You will be surprised what comes your way when you are open.

To live within your means you must know your income and your outgoings. The plan is to make sure your income is bigger than your outgoings. This means you can save money after you have taken care of your expenses. Once you have set up a budget for all the things you need to spend money on, you need to stick to it, however difficult this may be. Strong willpower and discipline will be needed and it is down to you alone to persevere.

CHAPTER 10

SHOWING OFF

A true hustler does not show off. There is nothing to prove to anyone and you should only be making money for yourself, family and friends. There is no need to show other people what you have got.

Showing off only makes sense if it is a tactic to attract potential business. There might be an occasion when showing off, or *'stunting'* as it is known on the streets, helps with your image. Success attracts more success so if you are celebrating because you have been successful, even if it is not completely true, it could make outsiders want to do business and share that success with you. However, in most cases showing off is usually a bad idea.

Everybody has times where they want to show off, especially to the opposite sex, and in this day and age, *'money talks'*. As a hustler you do need to have fun and enjoy yourself but you cannot get carried away with pleasure-seeking. As a man you might be in a club, for example, and spot a few ladies you want to go home with at the end of the night. After you have got their attention and had a little chat you might offer them a drink. The stunter, with his pocket full of cash, might buy them a bottle of champagne costing anything from £100 to £1,000 when he could have bought them a £5 glass of vodka and still got what he wanted at the end of the night. The point is live life but keep it under control.

A lot of people watch music videos and films and want to live the life they see on the screen. They hire rental cars and stunt in them for a weekend or two at £500 a time. They might do this 20 times over not realising that with the 10 grand they spent they could have bought the car they were renting if they had a little self-control or patience. The car would be theirs forever instead of stunting in it 20 times for a short-lived thrill. At the end of the day no one rates a stunter. The same man who rented the £100,000 plus sports car, cannot even get the girls a true hustler can pull in a cheap run-around. Real women will see through the fake image. When you hand back the keys of the rented car the girl you had does not want to know you anymore.

Stunters are fake hustlers. There are too many people who claim to be hustlers when really they are stunters and fronters who do not have a clue what to do with money. How many people do you know drive expensive cars but are still living with their parents? As a hustler you need to get your priorities in check. If you spend money on jewellery, clothes and luxury items, but have not moved out your parent's house, you need to evaluate your priorities. As a true hustler you must learn that no matter how much money you make it is what you do with it that counts. A lot of criminals dream of, and some actually do make, large lump sums of money, but when you have got £100,000 sitting under your bed in a shoebox what are your plans for it? The stunters and fake hustlers will go out and buy everything they think they need and maybe keep a little change for a rainy day. They continue to commit crimes and never really break the cycle of this type of existence. A hustler will take that same money and treat it like they have received a share from a private investor or a bank loan and they start a business with it. Hustling is a way to better your life and the people around you. Do not claim to be something you are not or live a lie. Be hungry but be humble.

THE SPOTLIGHT

Be careful of the spotlight. There are those who are naturally more popular than others either because of looks, stunting or reputation. This popularity makes the spotlight follow you. Everybody will want to know your business and get to know you. This can make you big-headed and distract you from what you are really trying to do, which is to make money. Do not stray off the path.

There is a story about the good looking, popular guy in school who was the centre of attention; he was in the spotlight all the time. He had nice clothes, was great at sports and had a name to live up to, but he spent too much time enjoying the attention he got from girls. It was only until he had his first child that he began to realise the importance and value of money. He had pulled off some big jobs and made a lot of cash, but attributing little value to the money, he continued to spend it all on jewellery, cars, and clothes. This boosted his popularity even more, but while he was enjoying the good life, local shottas who he had hardly noticed carried on grinding with no breaks. Before he knew it, these background guys had made huge sums of money and the spotlight had switched to them. The good looking popular guy had grown up. He had started a family but his constant concern with the spotlight and self-obsession had caused him to become broke. Life was now stressful and as a result of it all, his charm had faded; he did not look so good anymore.

Eventually you will lose the spotlight. As you get older you become more concerned with your own life; your family, your assets, your liabilities, your expenses. When young do not lose sight of the value of money and try not to get sidetracked when making it.

Do not stunt or show off. It is a dangerous game to play. It gives the impression to others that you have got plenty of money to waste. You will attract the evil eye; and the karma of continuously wasting money is never good. Remember, money equals food and much more. It pays for life's basic necessities. Squandering it on a daily basis will only create bad energy. Enjoy your money but be aware that there are people with a lot less. And as in the wild there are predators hanging around waiting to pounce, it might even be that a person in your close proximity, a friend, a partner or even a family member, is eyeing up what they can bleed from you. Stunting and showing off only attracts hate, jealousy and fake people. It may even kill you.

CHAPTER 11

DEBT

A hustler should try to avoid debt at all costs. Do not get into debt and if you are already in debt get out of it as soon as possible. Do not let people get into debt with you either because it creates complications, problems and drama. A famous old saying is, *'No man can respect you if you do not respect yourself and no man can respect himself if he does not or cannot repay honest debts.'*

There is such a thing as good debt. This entails borrowing money that you know you are going to use to make more. If you can do this successfully then it could be a good idea because you are making money without risking any of your own.

Learn to prioritise your debts. If you know you owe money to a certain person who is threatening you with violence or extortion, the wise thing to do is pay him or her first. As a hustler you need to learn how to avoid putting yourself into these types of situations. Borrowing money from the wrong type of person or company is not a smart thing to do. For example, your mortgage is a priority because if you do not pay it you could lose your house. Debts such as your phone or gas bill are important but not as serious as your mortgage.

The capitalist world relies on debts to function, from countries keeping other countries in debt down to the bankers keeping families and individuals in debt. Remember whoever controls the money has the power. The aim of the banks is to put everybody in debt. Governments are in debt to bankers and this should tell you where the power lies. Once you are in debt the banks can profit from the interest you pay repaying the borrowed money.

As a hustler you might have to borrow money but if you do so make sure you secure the best deal before you find yourself in serious debt, struggling to keep up. Everywhere you turn there are enticing offers of products or services you believe may benefit you. There are companies offering these on a '*buy now, pay later*' basis, however, do not fall for these illusions. They are simply other ways to get you into debt. You will be signed into a contract where you will pay more for a product or service than it is really worth. Be sure to always read the small print.

Very often legal small print fills page upon page because companies or manufacturers know it will be a hassle for you to read it all. This should not deter you. If you do not read the small print you will never fully understand the contract you are entering into, and if you do not understand a contract, then why would you sign it? As long as you are seen as credit worthy, most lenders will try their hardest to push loans and credit onto you, but only enter into debt if it is in your interest to do so.

If you are going to invest money you borrow to make more, with minimum risk, this could be a good way of making easy money. For example, if you know you could sell a car for £5,000 that you spotted someone selling for £3,000 and did not have any money to buy it, then this could be a situation where you could borrow money. You borrow the £3,000; sell the car for £5,000 making a £2,000 profit. You can then repay the £3,000 you borrowed giving some of your profit to the lender to show your appreciation.

There are dangers involved with borrowing and ticking money. You have got to be careful because if you do not repay the lender on time, you can create all kinds of problems for yourself. If you have borrowed from a company or bank you could be charged fines and interest, ruining your credit ratings as well. Bailiffs may even be sent to confiscate your possessions and valuables because of non-payment of money owed. If the lender is a person you know, you could lose a friendship, or be beaten up or extorted. None of these risks are worth taking. It is far better to be patient and save money in order to spend it.

If you are lending money make sure you receive some kind of collateral or reassurance. This is usually, or should be, something that is worth as much as the money you lent out. This lets you know your money will be repaid and if not you can sell what you have secured for the same amount. Always do this, even if someone has borrowed from you before and repaid you on time because it does not guarantee they will again. Some people might even try building a relationship with you, ticking all the time; then they will try to tick something big and have no intentions of paying you back. Remember even a friend or family member can bump you. It is just a harsh reality of life.

Tackling debt can be a difficult task because it requires you to make a surplus amount of money; money on top of what is needed to live on. Work out how much money you owe first, then prioritise the most important debts and do not forget to budget for essentials. Any extra money will be used towards repaying your debts.

Do not let the stress of debt effect your mind state. Share your problems with people close to you so the burden of it all does not get you down. Most importantly try not to get into debt in the first place.

CHAPTER 12

TRUST

Trust is not built, it is earned. It can take years to develop a trusting relationship, seconds to break it and a lifetime to repair it. Trust is a step-by-step process.

Guard your money at all times. Only keep money where you know it is safe. A lot of men keep stacks of money with a girlfriend, their baby's mother or a family member, but is your money really safe? All it takes is one argument and your stack could be gone. There is also the risk of them pinching a few pounds or more when they are in need. When you want your money back some may be missing and now you have to sort out how much was taken and owed. This is all unnecessary drama and can be avoided if you keep your money where you know it is safe.

Keeping your money or valuables at home can be a risky business because if the police ever have a reason to search your house and find it, you can be charged with money laundering unless you can explain where the money came from. There is always the risk of robberies too.

The obvious thing to do, it might seem, is to keep your savings in the bank. But to what extent can you trust the banks? Even these '*secure*' depositories come with their own risks. Banks can crash like any other businesses and money not insured by government policy can be lost. No bank is completely secure and people should not forget that a bank is just a business. Bank crashes can lose shareholders and investors money so it is advisable to find out what the amount of savings are that you can keep in a bank that will be covered by an insurance scheme. This means if the bank folds you can still recover your money. Anything over the amount will be lost so people with very large sums of money should spread their savings with different banks ensuring that their money is secure. Remember a bank makes money from your money so why not make money from your money too? Find out if buying assets will make you more money than keeping money in the bank. The answer will usually be yes. If someone has £200,000 in the bank, the annual interest might amount to a few hundred pounds but buying a house with this same amount of money might yield a rental income of a lot more, so be sure to do your homework. The bank is only your friend because you are making them money. They need you more than you need them. Without everyone's money they would not exist as a business. You have to decide which bank you trust the most and where your money will be at its safest.

Do not work or do business with someone you do not trust. If you have any negative feelings about a person or your natural instinct is telling you to avoid them, it is usually wise to listen because your gut feeling most of the time is right. It might be the person is a robber or a thief. They may be on the run from a crime or debt. They might have recently left prison and are hungry for money; also the police could be watching them. Just avoid conducting business with people you do not trust even if they are promising to repay you with interest on top. Untrustworthy people are usually good at lying and telling stories because they have been in these types of situations many times before. You are better off spending your money in a gambling house or on a shopping spree rather than letting someone else lose it for you.

Do not trust buying or investing in something just because the person or company selling it seems genuine. Never rush any purchases; always take your time to think about each individual one, comparing prices and quality. This will mean that you will be less likely to be ripped off. You will also be able to ensure the product you are buying is not defective in any way. Sales people and businesses will try to convince you that their product or service is the best, cheapest, and that you will not find better elsewhere, but do not trust them. Do your own investigations and research. If you do not have a history of doing business with that person or company, how can you trust them? They have to earn your trust.

When doing business in the streets you have to take even more precautions. Never put your money in someone else's hands until you can see and have examined the item you are buying. Hand over the money once you have your product. A famous gypsy hustle is to show a potential customer a product. When the deal is sorted and it comes to the exchange, the gypsies switch the bag or box with the product and take the money. They then make a hasty getaway and when the customer checks inside the packaging, instead of the valuable product they will find something cheap, like a bag of potatoes. Some drug dealers like to take money first and tell customers to wait while they go and get the product but are never to be seen again. So you cannot trust this arrangement. Even a hustler can get hustled.

If you do not trust someone make sure you do not bring them to where you live or work because there is always a risk they can rob you or reveal your plans to a competitor.

Trust and honesty are very important attributes to have as a hustler. People like to invest and work with someone who they can trust and rely upon. If you cannot be trusted your business deals will lead to nowhere; they will materialise into nothing so in the end you lose out. You must do everything you can to build an honest and trustworthy reputation. It will bring you respect, attract the best kind of business deals and associates; likely to take you to new heights of wealth and prosperity.

CHAPTER 13

OPPORTUNITIES

If you are to be a successful hustler you must learn how to recognise an opportunity when presented with one. Every problem has a solution and you must be able to spot this.

If you find an opportunity to make money and it feels right you should do your research and invest. Investing money always involves some risk but you have to weigh up whether the risk is worth what you might be rewarded with.

In the hustler's world there is no such thing as good luck. Good luck will only appear as an opportunity and it is you that needs to be able to see it. It is like the story about the man drowning in a flood, who believed that God would save him: a boat came by and one of its occupants invited him to climb aboard. The drowning man refused saying, '*God will rescue me.*' A little later a helicopter flew overhead. A ladder dropped down to the drowning man, with the pilot calling for him to climb aboard. The drowning man refused saying, '*God will rescue me*'. After the helicopter left the man drowned, died and went to heaven. Standing before God, the man asked, '*Why didn't you rescue me?*' God laughed and replied, '*I sent you a boat then a helicopter but you refused both.*' The moral is that an opportunity is only an opportunity if you can spot it in the crux of the moment.

Talking about something is different to taking action; and even when you spring into action be ready for the ups and downs. You might meet a person that is selling cheap electronic goods you know you can profit from. The seller is only going to have them for a short period, as demand is high. You should capitalise on this, making as much money as you can while they are around. A downer could be when a connect is going to prison so now you cannot get the cheap product you were being supplied with. In such situations you should use your hustling instincts to think quickly of a plan before you lose too much money. Even if you have to buy more expensive products elsewhere it would be wise to, so at least you can keep your clients happy and satisfied. When your connect finally comes back you have kept your business line going, so transactions can return to normal without you having lost any customers. Sometimes you will see someone miss money-making opportunities because they waste time doing something that could be done at any other time. The classic example is the man who spends too much time with his new girlfriend. He will never be a true hustler unless he sorts out his priorities. You may have a friend just like this. There might be an occasion when a move crops up and you ask your friend if they are interested, but you get the reply, '*No I'm with my girl.*' The move is a success and you make some money. When you next see your friend and he asks you to give him a little slice, all you should tell him is that you tried to involve him; if he declined the offer in the first place he does not deserve a cut so do not give him the time of day.

Often valuable time is wasted sitting around at home doing nothing. People are chilling all day long but an opportunity to make money does not come around that often. If your friends sincerely love you they will understand if you choose to go on a money-making venture rather than to hang out with them. Try to keep relationships separate to business.

Opportunities are missed as they can be disguised; it takes a real hustler to recognise when presented with one. Do not waste time waiting for opportunities as you can create them yourself by being positive and productive. Most people do not realise the great opportunities life

gives them until it is too late and then they have regrets. A negative thinker sees too many difficulties when an opportunity arises but a positive thinker creates opportunities from difficulty. Try never to be in a position where you regret the chances and opportunities you did not take in life. Seize the moment.

CHAPTER 14

RISK

Everybody takes risks in life but when it comes to money some people are a little more careful. As a hustler you need to be able to decide if a risk to make money is worth the consequences that might follow.

In the investment world you will hear it being said that, '*A small and safe return is better than taking a risky one*', or, '*Slow money is better than no money.*' For some people this might be true. If you are inexperienced or not willing to take a loss here and there, then go along with the status quo. But if you are trying to make serious money then you need to be able to take bigger risks. If you are willing to take these bigger risks then you need to take specialist advice in the field you will be investing in. You cannot expect to hold onto your money if you invest in something you have no idea about.

When you hear the word investment it is not necessarily a reference to just stocks and shares. It could be anything that you buy with the intention of selling to make a profit. Even when you buy a cheap laptop and then sell it on for more than you paid for it; that was an investment. If a dealer buys a product wholesale and then sells it at the market rate; that was also an investment.

Playing poker is a good way to learn how to weigh up risks as with each hand you play you have to gamble money to win, but with the possibility of losing it too. Try learning how to play. If you know how to already, try playing keeping in mind that every hand you play is like an investment.

As a hustler you can sometimes find yourself grinding and grafting on the wrong side of the law. For some hustlers this is preferable as money is made faster and is tax-free. If this applies to you, then you need to be aware of the risks you are taking. If you value your freedom more than your money then you should always stay on the straight and narrow. A regular job with a steady income would suit you better then one-off payments from risky deals no matter how vast the sum of money you have been told you will receive.

Certain hustlers who make their money illegally claim they make huge sums but in reality many of them would be making just as much on a legitimate wage job. Criminal hustlers who do actually make big money joke about this, but just remember the risks in hustling on the wrong side of the law are serious; they are no laughing matter. If things go wrong, you could end up in prison. If you are hustling illegally, ask yourself whether what you are doing is just too risky. Decide what risks you are willing to take. A person with nothing to lose can afford to take more risks than a person with much to lose. You have to know which one of these people you are.

Too many people are afraid of failure and this holds them back from their true potential. The biggest risk in life is to risk nothing at all. You have to be calculated and weigh up whether a risk you could take is worth the possible end result. You might fail, but only with failure can you learn not to make the same mistakes. True success cannot be fully appreciated without this. Each time you fail or take a step backwards, you are really taking two steps forwards for out of failure arises wisdom.

CHAPTER 15

THE MIDDLEMAN

The middleman, sometimes referred to as a go-between, is the person or company that introduces you to the buyer or seller. They usually want a fee for this introduction or will change the price of the products on sale without you knowing so they can make some profit themselves. Many wholesalers and companies will use a middleman because they just do not have the time or resources to reach the mass market.

Being the middleman can be great; you can make a lot of money just by knowing the sellers and the buyers. You can always make a drink. You find what a buyer wants for a cheaper price than what they are willing to pay. The difference in what they are willing to pay and how much you can get it for them, is the drink. For example, a friend wants to buy a television and tells you that they are willing to pay £400 for one. If you then find somebody who is selling the television your friend wants for £300, you can take your friend's £400, buy the television for £300, and keep the £100 profit as the drink.

Always go to source to purchase goods. Whether you are a diamond dealer, cocaine shotta or retailer, it is always the same: find out who is producing what you are selling to get the best price. This is known as cutting out the middleman. Most of the time someone, usually a company, is making a drink because sellers do not know where to buy products cheaper. Although cutting out the middleman can sometimes be difficult and complicated, or even dangerous, if you are able to do it safely and deal directly with the source of production, your profit margin will grow. Some hustlers are happy to use a middleman because it can save the time and energy spent searching for the product or service they want.

At times the middleman can be what holds a business relationship together. Once there was a boy who had a brother that got sent to prison. The brother met a Vietnamese man inside whose friends on the outside grew cannabis. The brother inside was eventually able to get a contact number for his brother on the outside to obtain these bricks of cannabis for an unbeatable price. However, the brother outside could not move these bricks by himself, for he did not have the required level of clientele for business of this scale, and so he asked a friend for help who in turn introduced him to his own friends, who began buying several bricks at a time. The brother outside began making good money and was able to drink his friend too. But he began to get greedy and decided to cut out his friend, the middleman. He began going directly to his friend's friends, gaining a larger drink by not having to share his profit with anyone. Eventually these customers realised that their good friend was not part of the business deals anymore. Without him, the brother outside lacked the same degree of street credibility he had once had. One day, the friends ordered two bricks but it was a ploy to teach the greedy brother a lesson. Not long after, the greedy brother received a phone call from the Vietnamese man in person, telling him that the money that had paid for the two bricks was counterfeit. The greedy brother lost out on a huge amount of money and his reputation was severely damaged. The moral of this story is you cannot always cut out the middleman. Sometimes they are there for your safety or benefit. They might be willing to deliver a product saving you time, money, reputation and risk of harm.

When purchasing goods, try to cut out the middleman; go to the source of production yourself as it will save you money, especially if the line in question is a regular one. However, if

it is not safe to do business in this way, if it will create problems you could do without, use a middleman. They could make your business deals flow smoothly. You must always stick to what you are comfortable with because when you conduct business in fear you will be completely disempowered; your deals can end before they even start.

CHAPTER 16

WORKERS AND BOSSES

In a business and as a hustler there are two types of people, the workers and the boss. You must distinguish which one you are. Remember that they both need each other; both play an important role. You cannot be a worker without a boss and you cannot be a boss without a worker. Both must play their position. A business will fail if the boss does not know how to lead his workers and if a boss has slacking workers you can expect the same thing to happen.

A lot of people let their pride and ego get the best of them and opt to be a boss but they do not have the skills or qualities to be at the top. Do not let pride get the better of you. If you are not a boss at heart do not try to be. You can still accumulate great money as a worker and usually with less stress. Decide what suits you best as this will help you to succeed. As a worker you can save money and one day open your own business where you will be the boss so to speak. All good bosses should have knowledge of what it is like to be a worker.

MAIN SKILLS AND QUALITIES NEEDED

MUSTS FOR THE BOSS:

◆ Must be able to lead

◆ Must have experience in the field that is being managed

◆ Must know how to control a business

◆ Must be able to make decisions sometimes on the spur of the moment

◆ Must be able to multitask

◆ Must show confidence at all times

◆ Must be able to think outside the box

THE WORKER MUST:

◆ Be able to follow and listen to instructions or directions

◆ Be able to use initiative where appropriate

◆ Be a good team player

◆ Be able to swallow pride if need be

♦ Be able to tackle obstacles mentally and physically

♦ Be able to maintain a good work ethic always

If you look at shotting as an example of a business environment, you will see both bosses and workers. Selecting the right role will usually determine how much money can be made because bosses are paid more than workers. If you are the boss more money will come your way. However, sometimes a worker can earn more than their boss as in the case of the shotta who is breaking down what their boss is giving to them and selling in smaller bits.

In order for a business to be a success, the boss and the workers must apply a strict work ethic. The boss must manage their workers and keep on top of things and the workers must work hard to make good money and not get fired.

The product or service a business delivers is not always determinate of that business's success. Typically, it is the workers who are selling the product or service who keep the business running and determine its success. As a boss you should always reward your workers if they have performed well. This keeps them dedicated and motivated. It gives them the incentive to always want to improve and perform to the best of their ability.

The boss of a business is only the boss if they do not need to be there constantly to run it. Other workers should be left in charge. If you have to work at your business more than you are away from it then it is more than a business; it is a job, a slog. Are you a boss or just the number one worker slogging away? A smart hustler will make other people work hard for them, including managers, although if you want to be a boss and run a successful business you must learn all about management skills and qualities. This goes for any business whether it is a drug empire or website. You must know how to manage the accounting, book keeping, marketing and employees. A hustler will set up a business and leave it to someone else to run but still collect money from it with the awareness that those left in charge will do their job or else risk being fired. Such a hustler may have various business ventures thus making them a packet. If you are a debt collector, for example, doing business for a number of companies, you should build a reputation of fear and respect around your name so effectively that a worker can collect your money for you just by whispering your name. If you are a shotta you should build up your clientele until it is good enough for a worker to take over and you can just collect money without moving from your chair. You should learn from these hustlers who exert little energy but at the same time are creating serious wealth.

Everybody wants to be a boss because of ego, arrogance and pride. But remember every boss was a worker at some stage. You will have to work to earn this title. You will have to learn to swim before you jump in at the deep end. When a ship is sinking the captain will ensure that the crew are rescued first. A good captain will be the last person to abandon ship. Being a boss, the captain, comes with responsibilities that not every hustler can handle.

CHAPTER 17

SETTING UP A BUSINESS

Many hustlers and other ambitious people believe that starting a business is easy but statistics show that over 50% of new businesses crash in their first year. This is generally because of failure to plan and lack of knowledge on behalf of the person laying the foundations of the business. A house built on shaky foundations will eventually fall down and the same is true of a business. There are simple steps that one should take in order to set up a business successfully.

THE SEVEN BASIC GUIDELINES

1. Generate an idea for your product or company. Do market research, and learn who your competitors are. Make sure you brainstorm everything about the ideas you have got. Focus groups are an effective way to work with potential clients and receive feedback on your idea so set one up.

2. Review all the ideas you have and discard all the poor ones before you commit and invest any time or money.

3. Now you have decided on your product you should begin to develop it, making sure to test it out. You need to identify your USP (unique selling point) and think about whom will be your target clientele. You should also think about how much it will cost to make your product. Get a patent for your product or idea so it cannot be copied.

4. Make a prototype. You should arrange a second focus group to discuss your product or idea with potential consumers. Afterwards you should access the feedback and make any necessary adjustments. Research information on packaging and storage.

5. Since you know all the details of how you are going to produce your product, including how much it will cost, you will now need to carry out a business analysis, estimating the likely selling price of the product based on your market research and feedback. Estimate how much you will need to begin to get it off the ground and what the break-even point and profit will be.

6. Your product or idea is now ready for the market. Everything must be finalized. You should be familiar with all the costs of production and resources. You should be having discussions with your manufacturer and supplier so you can arrange storage fees too.

7. The product or idea is ready to launch. You should begin to promote and advertise; then supply your customer's demand.

There are always risks when you start a business. Things to take into consideration include:

♦ Employees behaving unprofessionally or failing to meet the tasks you have set for them

♦ Loss of supplier or manufacturer

♦ Changes to laws and regulations that might affect your business

♦ Failure to plan for future problems or changes

♦ New competition

To counteract risk you can:

♦ Accept it

♦ Transfer it

♦ Reduce it

♦ Eliminate it

A business could accept a risk if the cost of reducing or eliminating it is too high. Risk can sometimes be reduced or eliminated by changing the way a business produces a product or delivers a service.

Once your business is set up and running there are six things you should remember if you want to provide the best service.

THE SIX RULES OF BUSINESS

1. TIMING - Consumers want you to be on time when delivering your product. When investing or selling, timing is everything, so make sure you know your product and market and be prepared to change with the times. If your business runs a service make sure you spend the right amount of time on a customer and it is not a rushed job.

2. QUALITY - It is simple: a consumer wants the best quality of a product or service otherwise they will go elsewhere.

3. QUANTITY - A consumer wants to get as much of a product as they can for the money they are prepared to pay for it.

4. PRICE - A consumer will always compare your price to your competitor's so do your best to price your product fairly. Do not price products or services too cheaply because you risk undervaluation, making consumers question the quality. Prices can change with demand. For example, if it is summer, selling a winter jacket may be difficult so you might need to drop your price. When winter arrives, the same jacket's demand will be higher so you can put the price back up.

5. RELATIONSHIPS - You should try to build a strong and friendly relationship with all customers. This will help to keep them returning. If you continue to treat customers with respect you will begin to have a customer base that is loyal to you, only using your product or service instead of your rival's. Be aware when a customer thinks you are a friend. They might just want a discount as well as freebies. If you feel they are taking advantage, remind them politely that you have a business to run, and must make a profit, but you are still giving them a good deal. If they are loyal, you could occasionally reward them with something extra because you know you will receive future business. In return, they may even promote your business through word of mouth.

6. CONSISTENCY - Once a customer uses your product or service and is satisfied, they return because they want exactly the same as they had before. Anything less and they will look at your competitors and see if they can provide a better service that is consistent; where prices hardly change and the quality of the product is never compromised.

Not meeting these six rules of business will inevitably cause your business venture to fail. If you stick to these rules your business is guaranteed to succeed.

CHAPTER 18

MONEY LAUNDERING

Money laundering is the process in which the proceeds of crime are transformed into legitimate money or assets. It is a way of hiding money you have made illegally. This money is called the proceeds of crime or 'dirty' money. After it has been laundered it can be called 'clean' money. This process is called 'washing', hence the term 'money laundering'. Money laundering was made illegal, as the aim is to take the profit away from crime. However, hundreds of billions of pounds are laundered through financial institutions every year.

Why is it an offence? If a person engaged in an arrangement knowingly involving money from the proceeds of crime, then that person is supporting criminal activity as they are helping criminals to profit from their crimes. In a court of law the prosecution will have to prove that the person had a requisite degree of knowledge, or they have to consider whether the suspects had obtained the money from the proceeds of crime, which could be hard to prove, but then again might not be.

There are usually three steps to money laundering:

THE THREE STEPS

1. PLACEMENT - Cash introduced into the system

2. LAYERING - Camouflaging the money to go unnoticed; hiding the illegal source

3. INTEGRATION - Generating a legitimate wealth from the illegal investments

Not all steps are needed if a different method is found to use the proceeds of a crime. An example of this is structuring which is the process by which money is broken into smaller amounts to avoid suspicion. Structuring is just a different form of money laundering.

Classic ways of laundering money involve the utilisation of one's job and taxes. A person could reduce the amount they take from their wage cheque and use the illegal cash they have instead, making sure they take small amounts now and again from their cheque account, to avoid any suspicion as to where money is coming from to live on. This is easy only with small amounts of illegal money. If someone is making large amounts of illegal money they need to think about creating a business that they could feed the money into. The business must have an untraceable method of making money. A cash-only car wash is a good example. The authorities may require that every car that uses it is counted but no one is checking this. This means it is not a problem if the car wash is not making much money or if it is making a lot of money; illegal sums the owner has from other sources could still be passed through the company's bank account without trace.

Some big companies as well as high-earning criminals prefer to deposit money in offshore bank accounts to avoid paying tax. Tax evasion is a type of money laundering. At the same time as investments are made overseas, in various tax-free states, the movement of this money goes unnoticed in the country of residence, where a high tax rate would normally be paid.

To become rich and successful is the aim of any hustler. However, if the money you make cannot be accounted for, you risk having your bank accounts and any other assets frozen by the authorities, until you can prove they were earned in a legitimate way. Being found guilty of

money laundering means you could very easily lose everything you worked so hard for.

CHAPTER 19

TAX

Tax is a charge imposed on people living under the rule of a *'powerful elite'*. Tax is never voluntary; it is always compulsory. In so called democracies these taxes are used to pay for public services. The people work and pay taxes which are collected by the authorities and then used by the government to spend on the people. There are only a few places left in the world that are tax free.

History shows that tax was first introduced when cities or states wanted to make revenue. When people entered and left cities they would be taxed on the goods they had, as usually they were there to buy and sell. This persists today, though more taxes have been introduced, as the powers that be recognise that taxation is a simple and extremely profitable way to make money. They keep the rich *'rich'*, and the poor *'poor'*. Tax paid to the state or government is used for public services and their upkeep. These services are usually free at the point of delivery but this might not be the case in the future as many public services are being privatised. It is possible that in years to come there could be call-out charges introduced. Dialling an emergency service and being asked for a payment before anybody is sent to help, or being sent a bill after the call-out, could soon become a reality, which means only those with a lot of money will get the care they need.

Services that are usually free, as a result of taxes, are the fire brigade, the police, the armed forces and some health care provision, depending upon the country. Tax payer's money also goes towards the building and maintenance of roads and any public buildings. Some countries give money in the form of benefits to its citizens from taxes, but despite these benefits, taxes are generally unpopular because of the sheer amount of them. Moreover, the money paid in taxes is far greater than the money spent by the government; in other words money is being pocketed somewhere.

There are various types of tax and if you want to stay on the right side of the law you must pay them when required to. If you do not you could be caught and sent to prison. As a hustler it is important to familiarise yourself with taxes and how to keep the majority of your money. Different countries around the world have their own methods of collecting tax and some countries are supposedly tax free. However, their governing bodies just collect this money elsewhere to compensate themselves. Often, those residing in these countries pay higher prices on other things, so in effect they are still being taxed.

INCOME TAX

This is a tax from your income. You are required to give a percentage of the money you make from working as income tax. The more money you earn the higher the percentage. If you work for somebody else or for yourself, you still have to pay taxes on your income. So whether you make a lot of money or a little money, you are still a slave to your government.

The money you earn is all gross, meaning no tax has been deducted. You then pay taxes and the money left is your net profit. It is extremely important to stay on top of your accounts, and if you are not competent, hire an accountant. As a hustler you should try to manage your own accounts. Keep a business account or some sort of record of all money you spend and receive.

If you are employed by someone else usually they will deduct the tax for you and you just receive your salary for the work you have done. If you are a boss or self-employed you will be responsible for paying your own taxes. You will need to keep records of everything you do. Your expenses can be deducted and usually compensated for, so smart hustlers will make sure they keep records. The less tax you pay the more money you keep. This is not breaking the law; it is just merely taking advantage of it. Remember the government wants as much money as they can get from you, so you need to make sure you can cover yourself; you must be able to explain all of your accounts and bookkeeping.

CAPITAL GAINS TAX

This is a tax on any assets sold. When you sell an asset or investment you will be taxed for any increases in the original price you bought it for. There is an allowance that is renewed annually, so if your profit is below this allowance, you will not be taxed.

INHERITANCE TAX

This is a tax on any money or assets left after death. This tax is seen by many as an illegal tax because if someone has already paid income tax their entire life, they should not be taxed again after death.

ROAD TAX

This is a tax for drivers. Different countries have different laws and regulations but road tax is usually a tax on motor vehicles that drive on public roads. As a hustler you must be aware of all the costs and the responsibility involved in registering a vehicle in your own name. Parking in the wrong place can often result in a penalty charge but a good hustler will be knowledgeable of the law surrounding tickets, penalty notices and fines. Often the language used in these is an indication as to whether the charge is lawful or unlawful and many drivers end up paying money to companies that have no real lawful authority. Most penalty charges are an illegal tax and a good hustler will never give away their hard-earned money to daylight thieves.

On the streets some criminals try to take advantage of smaller criminals or legitimate businesses and charge them a tax. This is a form of racketeering or extortion. It is illegal but it goes on. These criminals or racketeers are no different to the government officials. Whether the criminals or the government are paid, it does not make a difference; people will have the same feeling of being oppressed when they pay tax to anyone.

As a hustler who is making money you must be aware that you could become the target of extortion.

Try to avoid this at all costs. Some criminals will offer protection for the tax paid to them. In many poverty-stricken neighbourhoods where criminals have power, owners of businesses will pay taxes or extortion money to keep their business safe. It is arguable whether these taxes are any different to those paid to a government who sets in place a police force to protect business, pointing to the fact that the police are in a way gangsters too. They enforce rules and collect taxes for governments and the elite. They do not serve and protect the general public; ordinary citizens are just not on their agenda.

Tax will always exist in a controlled society. Even when the majority of public services are funded by private business, the elite still tax the people. Government policy can bring about change in the tax system, however, this will only happen if people push ministers to act. Since '*money talks*', poorer people are at a disadvantage, but those who are rich are heard. The rich instigate change or buy it. The poor can do the same if they pool their resources; acting together they can be a stronger force when saying no to unjust taxes.

CHAPTER 20

CRIME PAYS

Crime is a by-product of money. Most crime is fuelled by the want or lack of money. There are few societies in the modern world that are not reliant upon money, and in turn there are not many societies unaffected by crime. Crime goes hand in hand with money. This begs the question as to whether capitalism, consumerism and Western society more generally, can even exist without crime. Many occupations encompass some type of criminal act, or serve as a crime-related service, and so without crime, these occupations would be obsolete. The armed forces commit crimes that go unpunished every day. Murder, violence and robbery are all part of the job. The police force would not exist if there was no crime. Half of the judicial systems across the world would be out of work. There would be no need for security. Without crime there would be no prisons, and, whether state-run or private, these institutions require the continuation of

crime to provide inmates for cheap labour. Crime is just big business. Criminality is far from ideal but it serves as a support mechanism to the system. As a hustler try to avoid prison at all costs. They say, *'time is money'* so a loss of time is a loss of money.

Everybody likes making money and there are so many different ways to accomplish this. Consider whether you want to be a hustler who hustles on the wrong side of the law. Most of the original hustlers were lawbreakers. As a conscious person it is important to decipher between what is right and wrong. Just because you hustle on the right side of the law does not mean what you are doing is necessarily right. Soldiers, for example, are paid wages for killing human beings; robbing and pilfering from other countries. This might be lawful but is it right? Police officers are paid to uphold the law but form part of an institution that is largely racist and very often corrupt. Is this right? Working for a bank is a lawful job but banks are responsible for keeping people oppressed and putting people in debt. Is that right? Breaking the law is in no way a better option than remaining lawful but as a hustler you must be fully conscious and decide what feels best for your spirit. Make money whilst having compassion for others. Always consider how what you do can affect other people.

Some of the advantages of not following the law are as follows:

♦ You choose when you work

♦ You may not need qualifications

♦ You do not have to pay tax

♦ You have cash in hand so can spend spontaneously

♦ You feel you have succeeded; as if you have made something of yourself out of nothing

♦ A feeling of power arises

The disadvantages of breaking the law are as follows:

♦ You always have to look over your shoulder

♦ Your money is dirty money so you will need an explanation as to where it came from or it can be confiscated as the proceeds of crime

♦ If caught, you could be taken into custody, the length of time being dependent on the crime

♦ You may have to live with a guilty conscience

♦ Family ties may be severed

♦ Your reputation could suffer

There are many different criminals:

FRAUDSTERS

Fraud is criminal deception with the intention of gaining an advantage. Fraudsters are sometimes referred to as swindlers. Fraudsters can make money with just a few phone calls, meetings and paperwork. Usually a fraudster's victim is not confronted or seen, lessening the guilt a fraudster feels about what they are doing. It is a cleaner crime when compared with other crimes that may involve physical violence. There are always new methods of fraud as one can themselves make up a way to defraud someone. In time, fellow fraudsters will catch on to this new method, sharing it with others, and so it goes on. Fraudsters are usually trying to find a way to sell something to someone, only the thing they allege to be selling either does not exist or they do not plan on giving it to the victim once the payment has been received. Fraudsters make false claims to accomplish what they want to do and sometimes they use other people's identities to steal their money. There are companies that operate under the law that also use the same tactics as fraudsters. Many sales companies use fraudulent sales techniques and get away with it; they dupe customers no end.

SHOTTAS

Shottas, otherwise known as drug dealers, are individuals that sell illegal substances for recreational purposes. This is an easy career to start as all you need is a phone, a little cash to buy a product and a few customers. The limit of where you go from there is up to you. In Chapter 17, 'Setting up a Business', the six rules to business are applicable to shotting just like with any other business. Being a shotta, assuming you are the boss and not working for someone else, it is almost as if you are running a business: you buy your product in bulk and break it down into smaller bits to sell on. Usually the bigger the amount you buy, the cheaper you will get it, increasing your profit margin. It is important to find the best connections to do this. Location is significant too, as you need to know if there are a lot of potential customers in the area you plan to set up in. You might be treading on someone else's turf and this could cause drama you do not want. There is always a place you can shot hassle-free so your only worry need be the police. You may require some kind of muscle or protection as you can become a target to robbers and extorters depending how much money you make. A good shotta will not meet their customers in the same spot regularly as the authorities are never far behind. Good shottas do not let random customers call their line as they never know who it might be. They will refrain from doing business with anyone, be it customers or connects, unless they have checked them out beforehand. The aim is to stay safe, even at the top end of the game. Since there will always be competitors and traitors, the six rules of business must apply.

ROBBERS

They deprive people wrongfully and forcibly. They steal from a person or business, aggravating through violence or intimidation. This is the high end of the criminal world as they are considered more dangerous than most other criminals. Robbery always has a victim or victims who are confronted and sometimes forced or threatened into handing over belongings or valuables they are in possession of or protecting. Smart robbers will always think about get away vehicles, changing clothes, wearing gloves and a disguise, and a safe house where they can store and count what they have taken. The police are never far behind so they must plan what they are doing carefully. However, with planning comes added years to the sentence if caught, for this is considered 'conspiracy'.

EXTORTERS

An extorter is someone who practises extortion. Extortion is the illegal securing of money by compulsion of violence. It can be an easy way to make money as sometimes not a lot of effort is needed. There could be serious repercussions though, because an extorter is taking hard-earned money from people, and nobody gives up their money without a fight. The extorter uses force, violence, bribery, threatening behaviour and reputation to make other hustlers and money-makers hand over their cash. This could be on a regular basis or just a one off payment. Extorters often need muscle or a serious reputation because no one would just give over cash if they did not have to. Extorters stand at risk of retaliation so they have to stay on guard.

INFORMANTS

Hustlers on the wrong side of the law always have to watch out for informants. An informant is a person who gives information to the authorities. These individuals are the worst of the worst, the snitches, the grasses, the rats. You will never know who is capable of doing this until a situation arises. Under pressure or for money, many people can turn on one another. A lot of so-called gangsters and hustlers turn snitch because of selfishness and fear of prison.

It is smart to keep business to oneself. Only a tight circle of people around you should be trusted. To be completely safe in business you should trust no one. Always move with precaution. Snitches are usually selfish and greedy people. They ask too many questions and try to get too friendly too quickly. It is possible they can wear some kind of recording device to gain incriminating information. The police might use them to do some kind of sting operation where they will attempt to catch you in the course of a criminal act.

TAKING PRECAUTION

♦ Talk in codes

♦ Always double check things including people

♦ Investigate individuals you are working with

♦ Change phones and numbers regularly

♦ Do not shit on your own doorstep

♦ Use an alias name so you do not put yourself on the radar

♦ Do not meet in the same places

♦ Do not keep anything illegal where you rest your head

◆ Destroy any incriminating evidence

People are products of their environment. Therefore, poor neighbourhoods will always breed crime. As a hustler you must realise there is no difference between some people who break the law and some who abide by it. Usually people who break the law are prepared to take more risks; they will grab an opportunity whenever they see it coming. These so-called lawbreakers live on the edge of society and because this has its own appeal, making the transformation to becoming legit or fitting in is hard. However, hustling on the right side of the law is a lot less stressful; so aim to do this. Crime pays but freedom is priceless.

CHAPTER 21

THE AUTHORITIES

Hustlers should be aware that they are being watched, observed and analysed more than they realise. All types of technology and methods are used to pry into people's private lives and business. Any slip-ups and a hustler could be answering questions that their future could depend upon. Failing to stay ahead of the authorities, or not taking the right precautions in business, could result in having to answer to the powers that be; even losing liberty and freedom.

The police are often described as an organisation set up to serve and protect the public. In actual fact they are an organisation set up to serve and protect finances. Ever wondered why there are more police in a thriving city centre than a poor neighbourhood? This is because police protect money. Often deprived neighbourhoods are poorly policed because nobody from these neighbourhoods pays the police. The police will only get paid for the criminals they catch and prosecute. In wealthy areas there are more police because there is more money; it is that simple. Where business thrives and where money is made, there is always a higher level of security. Even crime is measured in costs: a paedophile or rapist has committed far worse crimes than someone who sells drugs. However, in cases of drug dealing where dealers are making a racket, the law looks upon this as the greater crime and the sentence handed out is usually longer. Trials that can make money, just by their very nature, are murder cases. These are considered the ultimate crimes by the judicial system. They result in a payday for everybody; more work is entailed so there is more money to go around. As a hustler you must be aware that the more money you make the more you will be watched.

UNDER-COVER POLICE

One of the tactics the police use is an 'under-cover' officer or agent who will dress in plain clothes trying to portray the identity of a criminal so as to go deeper into the criminal underground. Pretending to be this person, they will attempt to catch as many criminals as possible. They might try to buy drugs, weapons and anything else illegal. Some undercover officers have been known to build a criminal identity for years in order to infiltrate gangs; making themselves even harder to detect. Hustlers must be aware of who they work with or deal with. When meeting new contacts they must ask themselves questions: how did I meet this person? Who are they associated with? Can they be trusted? They need to investigate the people they do business with. In the same way a legitimate business will interview new employees, a similar process must take place on the streets. Try to get a reference from somebody who has conducted business with that person in the past and can vouch for them. These precautions will save you from doing business with under-cover police and anyone else who may pose a threat to your freedom.

SURVEILLANCE

Close observation, or what is sometimes referred to as '*under obo*', is simply the sizing up of a suspect or suspects. If a person is seriously suspected of dealing in any illegal activity, the police might put them under surveillance to catch them out. They will keep a watchful eye on every aspect of a suspect's life, to build a portfolio of incriminating evidence, to be used later in a court of law, to prosecute. Photos or video recordings are taken. Close friends and associates, including family members, may be scrutinised. Cars the suspect drives, or places they reside in, are thoroughly checked over. Phone calls are listened into and bugs are placed in many places, to capture a bigger picture, to be exhibited at some point, in front of a judge and jury. This process can last a long time; sometimes for years. Once someone is under obo, it is highly likely that they will be sent to prison for a very long time.

Hustlers should be aware that surveillance does not only come in the form of CCTV and watching someone physically; if under surveillance it is likely your use of the internet is also being monitored. Not only are criminals observed in this way but ordinary citizen's private lives are being pried into as well. Companies monitor people's internet use and shopping patterns for marketing and financial reasons. As a hustler always be on point and do things with a mind that one is constantly being watched.

BUGS

Bugs are hidden electronic devices that can capture video evidence or record verbal evidence; they can even track movements. They transmit data to a receiver. The authorities have the technology to remotely activate the microphone in your mobile phone to listen in to conversations. People assume the methods they see the police using to catch criminals in the films are fake but they are all real. Police have the best technology out there at their disposal. They will put bugs in your home, car and phones if they suspect you of a crime. They can listen to any of your conversations and track any of your movements. It costs money to do this but they make a lot more money if they catch you, so it is worth their while. If you are on their radar and they target you, they will go to extreme lengths to make sure you are caught. Do not expect to hear a crackling sound if your phone has been tapped. This is just an urban myth. Technology has advanced to the point where you will hear nothing.

LAWYERS

Lawyers act for both the authorities and individuals. The authorities use lawyers to prosecute and individuals use lawyers to defend themselves. Sometimes it is the other way around but this is a lot less often. Lawyers are those who have studied the law of the land and understand the language used in law. The language of law is quite different to the language used every day and this is to confuse the average person. As a hustler you must educate yourself; learn the language of law so that you can defend yourself if a situation may arise. Do not just rely on a lawyer. A good businessman has a competent understanding of accounts and maths; he does not just rely on his accountant. It is the same for the hustler. If you find yourself in a lawsuit you should understand the language that will be used in the courtroom. Life is a like a game of chess. The same pieces in a chess game make the same moves regardless of colour or of the fact that they are on opposing sides. In life the same professionals will also carry out the same moves regardless of colour, race, gender and the side they are on. This means you can hire a lawyer but that does not mean they are working for you. Whether they are acting for the defence or the prosecution, lawyers are playing in the same game. Do not play games with your life, your money or your freedom. Interview and investigate the lawyer you hire. Do not simply accept any lawyer given to you. If you do not know them, how can you trust them? Lawyers make private deals and are part of a corrupt system that is outdated and racist. Money controls the law so the less money you have, the harder you have to fight if you find yourself in a lawsuit.

The authorities are there to keep order and stop chaos. Whether you side with the authorities or not, you must realise that it is all just business. If you move in the correct manner you will give the authorities no reason to notice or hassle you. In the past there were slaves who whipped other slaves but they were all still slaves. Hustling can set you free.

CHAPTER 22

ECONOMICS

Economics is a social science that studies how individuals and groups of people govern and allocate funds and resources within a society.

The way people live amongst one another is constantly changing, and as the world evolves, so too does economics. In order to prosper as a hustler you must understand and study economics carefully.

To get to grips with economics, you must first consider human behaviour, which requires starting with basic science. When stripped of clothes and material possessions, humans are little different to the other creatures that inhabit the earth. Human beings eat, sleep, work, socialise, reproduce and try to find time to enjoy life whilst doing these things. What separates human beings from the rest of the animal kingdom is intelligence and spirituality. Biologically, humans come in all different shapes and sizes. Every human is different and yet every human shares basic biological DNA. The human family share the planet earth; each human taking in oxygen to breathe, and food and water for fuel. These are the basic necessities of human life, but with an ever growing planetary population, these necessities are not guaranteed.

As the world evolved, so too did humans, migrating to all corners of the earth. At some point in history people started sharing less and competing more; competing to the extent where devastating wars were fought between great nations over finances and power. Precious resources were stolen and innocent blood shed, all of which continues to this very day. The current situation is this; a handful of super-rich families control the financial arena, manipulating the world's banks and holding governments to ransom. Despite this elite grasp upon the world's economics, it is important to remember that nobody can control an individual's soul. No matter how much these elitist puppeteers may try, they will not succeed.

How are you affected as a hustler; an individual trying to make a good living? First you must evaluate where you fit into the world scheme of things. What are your goals? Are you here to compete or to share? Hustling in itself is quite competitive but this does not mean that you cannot share your achievements and triumphs with others; support your friends and family with your profits and build a network around you that will create an energy force that provides you and them with everything you all could possibly need. The most successful people on the planet, as competitive as they might seem, had to share in order to prosper. If you are a seller, anything you are selling is worthless without a buyer, so already this involves sharing. Sharing does not have to mean giving away something for free; and sharing can be sharing an idea or sharing energy. If you study science you will understand that everything is made up of energy and that all things share basic similarities. Today's currency is fiat money, but do not be fooled; currency has no real value. Its value is determined by the energy and value a person gives it. Paper money has no life; it cannot bring life but the energy involved in working or hustling for that piece of paper is its value. An exchange of energy has to happen. The work or service or goods sold, and therefore shared, consists of the energy of a particular interaction and in return you can then use the paper money to get what you need.

The problematic concept of modern fiat money has left many people trapped in a state of financial enslavement. Obtaining what you require using less energy is the path to financial emancipation. To preserve your energy is freedom. However, this is hard to do on your own. Preserving energy is easier to achieve collectively, and so sharing is the most effective formula to prosper.

Identify who makes up your network and begin building upon the relationships which constitute this network. This means looking at where you live. You will have a family, an extended family, friends, and distant relatives; this is your immediate circle. Then each of the people in your circle will have their own immediate circles. These circles become a network and networks become communities. As a hustler you must spend your money within your circle first. Then you can spend money within your network. If you spend outside of the network that money is lost. This type of economic spending is a form of communal economics similar to Susu economics, a form of banking that goes on in West Africa. The money goes round in a circle never leaving the circle, and so is never lost. This method of economics preserves your energy. This is a recipe for success and many communities thrive using this formula.

If you decide to go it alone you must remember that it will be a lonely path. Hustling should always be fun and fulfilling, earning money in a righteous way in order to experience a better standard of living. Anything you do for money but fail to enjoy is soul destroying. The world today is so competitive that people are becoming more and more unconscious. Competition has got to the stage where human beings are so divided they no longer act as one human family. There is infighting sometimes over things that do not matter. People are killing to eat like they are in a concrete jungle.

POLITICS

How does economics relate to politics? You must understand the system you live in. You may think that if you get political power you will get economic power, but this is not true as money is the power. Money funds things. It is the fuel or the energy that everything uses. A government does nothing; it merely governs the money of the people, that which holds the real power. Therefore, if a government borrows money from a bank, who is it that has the power? The bank of course. Hustlers should never get sidetracked with politics. Make money first and then decide where you want to pledge your allegiance.

UNIONS

A union is the act of joining together. In an economic context this usually happens to protect one another: strength in numbers and strength in unity. Politics is a numbers game, and in any business, company or organisation, having unified numbers working together is powerful. When union members pay money into their union this money becomes financial power.

The economy is not something static. It continually changes. Fiat money in the form of cash money is slowly disappearing and most money is just numbers on a screen. Bank cards and credit cards are used more than cash now and there are already places in the world where people have their bank details and personal information put onto micro-chips and inserted into their body. As a hustler you should be ready for any changes but a discerning hustler will manipulate change itself. Understand you have the power to be part of the bigger picture. What you do today affects your future. Unity is power. The future is constantly changing but nothing is ever certain. Unifying with people of like mind will help you to have some say in how the future of money is heading.

The only way to affect or change the economy is to begin with yourself. Study yourself as well as the economy. Start to self-reflect. Realise that it is you the individual who has the capacity to progress and instigate change for the better. Then join together with others who think the same. Power to the people; power to the hustler.

CHAPTER 23

THE ANIMAL KINGDOM

The world with all its technology and constant changes and advances is still just an animal kingdom. Humans no matter how civilized they try to be, all share basic human nature. This nature is what unifies but separates at the same time. It is survival of the fittest. In order to be fit an individual must be aware of their surroundings, understand nature and most importantly understand themselves. They should be in touch with the spirit inside. Animal instinct is what separates the strong from the weak. If people lose touch with their animal instinct they can find themselves at the mercy of fitter humans. As a hustler you must always be aware you are in an animal kingdom. Like the tiger that goes out and hunts for meat to bring home for its family, or for itself, you must do the same, only the meat you are pursuing is money. You should aim to be like a tiger; unnoticed, always aware of what others are doing, but not interested unless it will affect their own self. This is not selfishness but self-preservation perfected. The tiger is regarded by many cultures as a very spiritual animal. A famous saying is this: '*It is better to live one day as a tiger than a thousand years as a sheep*'. Do not follow blindly; always be aware and conscious. You will encounter many different humans along your journey in life and you will notice the spirit of certain animals inside of them. If you are aware of this and are able to spot a human's animal spirit, it may help you not only to survive but to prosper.

ANIMALS

SNAKES - Humans with this spirit are very sly. They can be difficult to identify because they may act like your friend when in reality they are not. You can never trust such a person. Given the chance they will set you up for failure or for your demise. Just as the snake approaches its prey silently when going for the kill, the snakes of the hustling world handle their business in the same way. If you do not see them coming, it could already be too late.

CATS - Humans labelled '*cats*' on the streets are usually addicts. A cat will always come back for more. Throughout history, cats have been observed by humans. They have no loyalty to the human race. This often led humans to believe cats were special creatures. In this modern era, cats are just customers; they are good for selling things to. They might bring you valuables and products for cheap prices but they like to gossip and cannot be trusted. Any human that moves like a cat has no loyalty, although they can be good to have around because they will always want whatever you have to offer. Remember a tiger is a large cat. Understand this and be aware of such power and you will be able to control small cats to your advantage in the hustling world.

RATS - Humans that act like rats are gossipers. Rats will report or *'rat'* on others to the authorities, or to other hustlers. Rats attempt to bring others down and take over. If you surround yourself with rats or let a rat into your home you can be sure that they will share any information with rivals, potential robbers and even the police. The rat survives by scavenging. It is a scavenger by nature. In the business sector a rat in your business could hack through your emails and share them with a rival company. Rats bring information to the pigs so be careful not to let them know your business.

PIGS - Most people know who the pigs are: the police. Humans with this spirit are usually very weak-minded and this is why police just do as they are told by the powers to be. Do not underestimate the pig. In the wild a pig would be no match for a tiger but pigs will use all the other animals to bring down the tiger. They will use the snakes, the rats, the cats and even the dogs. They cannot be stopped so try to avoid them completely. As a spiritual human being it is good to respect all animals but at the same time respect those who respect themselves. Pigs eat their own faeces and so this shows you the level of respect they deserve.

DOGS – A lot of men have the spirit of a dog. It is quite common. Unlike cats, dogs can be trained to become loyal. However, a dog is only loyal to the person who feeds it. If you have dogs around you, make sure you feed them or they will bite you. Although it is said that you, '*should not bite the hand that feeds you*', if you have a dog and do not feed it for a few days, you will see just how aggressive it can become. There was once a hustler who when going to the local fast food shop would notice that a lot of his boys (dogs) were so broke they could not even buy food. This hustler, whenever he bought a meal for himself, would make sure he bought meals for all his dogs too. Some might say that is money wasted, but to him, as a hustler, it was money invested. Once this hustler was getting chased by the police and the drugs on his person could have put him in prison for many years. He ran past the shop where his boys hung out and when they noticed the police in pursuit, they told him to give the drugs over to them for safekeeping. By feeding his dogs (the boys) a couple of meals, they had saved him from doing time. Not only did they save him that day, but on other days they would bring him money-making opportunities instead of approaching other hustlers. Dogs remain loyal to whoever feeds them the most.

SHEEP - These are followers. Sheep only follow other sheep. A sheep will not follow a tiger so you cannot expect much from sheep. To engage a sheep and make this person useful, you must make them aware of their spirit and help them to adopt a new one, if this is someone you wish to have a close business relationship with. Sheep are scared creatures and this is why they move in large numbers and follow one another. It is just for safety. In the financial world sheep are the consumers, the masses. As a hustler, if you are selling a product, you must market this product to the sheep.

CHAMELEONS - They can adapt to a situation or their surroundings. This is a great characteristic to have and whatever animal you think you are similar too, you should try to practice being a chameleon so you can deal with any situation or surroundings you find yourself in.

PEACOCKS - Humans that have this spirit are flamboyant people; show offs. The male peacock and female peacock differ. The male shows off to attract the female. A woman that has this peacock spirit will be attracted to men that show off their wealth. Peacocks look fancy but in the animal kingdom they are not the real hustlers. They only look good to other peacocks.

LIONS - Most humans aspire to be a lion because the lion is the king of the jungle. Humans that possess the nature of a lion are usually leaders. They are very family orientated and have a lot of pride. In business someone of this nature is usually a boss. A lion and a tiger are virtually equal in strength and power but where they differ is their journey in life; the lion usually works better in a team whereas the tiger works better alone.

BUTTERFLY - The butterfly was once a caterpillar. Humans with this spirit have made a personal transformation and this person is usually content. They do not care about money and material things. They have reached the final point in life where they now show off their achievements but in an altruistic way. The butterfly in nature represents enlightenment and perfection; once asleep they are now awake.

There are many more animals in the animal kingdom that a hustler should be aware of. Understand the characteristics of the people you

encounter and observe nature carefully for this will help you to achieve success. Be careful because a lot of animals that present themselves to you will not be the animals they appear to be. A natural instinct in the wild and a defence strategy is that animals try to camouflage their appearance or they will hide away. Likewise, humans will do the same. When talking to people they will subconsciously hide their true nature from you unless they feel you are a friend. As a hustler you must be able to spot a person's true nature if you want to conquer this animal kingdom. Keep in mind the concrete jungle; you have to be consciously fit to survive.

CHAPTER 24

RULES OF THE GAME

As a hustler there are some fundamental rules one should follow if one intends to become rich and successful. Some people like to live life with no rules, and in certain circumstances this can be perfectly fine; rules do not always have to be followed and there is no rule to say one rule is better than another. As a hustler one must be at least aware of the unwritten rules that have helped the hustlers who have come before them achieve success. Every action has a reaction and every rule was devised for a reason.

RULES

1. KNOWLEDGE - Always try to expand your knowledge, particularly the knowledge related to money. How can you make money if you do not understand it? Read books, go to seminars, and speak to the rich and successful. You can never know enough. A very wise hustler once said that you should, '*Live, love, learn and grow*', and that is exactly what you should do when hustling. A great way of learning more about money is to find a mentor, someone you can spend time with who will guide you and teach you what they know. Try to find someone who has done what you are trying to do. They will have the knowledge you need. The wise hustler also said that, '*You are only as good as the five people you spend your most time with*'. If you surround yourself with people who do not do anything productive, who never make a penny, this will reflect on you. If the five people closest to you are not wasting time doing nothing, if they are making a good living, then you can expect the same too. If you have to change the five then so be it; and if it means spending less time with a friend, then you have to do what you have got to do. If your friend is authentic they will understand your intentions. Do not let anyone hold you back. It is a good idea to surround yourself with people who will drive, motivate and push you to make money in a legit way. They should be willing to sacrifice their time to help you. Knowledge separates the rich from the poor; a hustler should always be striving to increase their knowledge.

2. DO NOT GET INTO DEBT - You should avoid borrowing money from a company or person unless you are going to invest it to make more. If you are already in debt then make it a priority to clear the debt as soon as possible, to become debt-free. The reverse is also true; do not let others get into debt with you. Even if you are making money through lending, eventually you will lose money because the probability is that some people will not repay their debts; they will slip away.

3. REPUTATION - When hustling you should build and maintain a good reputation. Always be honest and loyal. More business will come your way in the long run and you will not have to live your life looking over your shoulder. Many fake hustlers are greedy and will sacrifice a richer tomorrow for a little cash today. If people know you are someone who can be trusted and that you have a good reputation, they will want to work with you. Take care of your friends and family because you never know when you might need them.

4. SAVE MONEY - A wise hustler should always save money. Money should be put aside for investments, the future and as a safety net for any difficult financial times ahead. You need to have at least three different stacks of money saved; investment stacks, future stacks and safety stacks. Your available cash and available funds should be kept separate from your savings. Do not dip into savings for everyday usage or living expenses. A safety stack is like insurance for oneself. If something goes wrong and you suddenly find yourself searching for funds to fix or pay for something, these funds will be available from your safety net that is stacked away. An investment stack is useful because you never know what investment opportunities may arise. You will need readily available funds and this stack will fulfil this purpose. The future stack covers almost everything else and should never really be touched so that it constantly grows. You will never know in the future how this money could help you.

5. AWARENESS - Being aware is extremely important, however, a lot of people do not realise this. Being aware as a hustler means protecting your finances; guarding your money. You need to keep your money where you know it is safe. Protect your money and valuables because there will always be people out there who want to take it off you. There are hundreds of people who want to get their hands on your money. They come in all shapes and sizes and will go to crazy and imaginative lengths to do so. They might be conmen, robbers, extorters or jealous friends. Watch out for the criminals but keep an extra eye open for the taxmen and the government who can take your money legally.

RULES

1. Always increase your knowledge.

2. Do not get into debt or let others get into debt with you.

3. Build a strong and honest hustling reputation.

4. Make sure your savings are growing.

5. Be aware of and protect your finances.

CHAPTER 25

FINANCIAL WORDS AND MEANINGS

Here are some financial words and meanings that could be useful.

ASSET - A useful or valuable thing or person, something that brings you an income.

BALANCE - The total amount of money you have in the bank or owe to a lender.

BANK - Business entity formed to maintain savings and checking accounts, issue loans and credit, and deal in negotiable securities issued by government agencies and by corporations. Banks are strictly regulated and fall into the following three categories according to the legal limitations upon their activities: commercial bank, savings and loan association, savings bank.

BOND - An investment where you lend money.

CAPITAL GAINS TAX (CGT) - The tax paid on any increases of an asset when it is sold.

COLLATERAL - The security asked for when a lender is issuing a loan. Sometimes this could be your home or something of similar value to how much money you are trying to borrow.

COMMODITY - Any tangible good or product that is the subject of sale or barter. Bulk goods such as grains, metals and foods are traded on a commodities exchange or spot market.

COMPOUND INTEREST - Interest paid on interest. If a bank pays you this, your savings will increase faster.

CONSOLIDATION LOAN - A loan used to repay other loans. If a person owes money to many different companies, they can get this to pay them all at once in a larger payment.

CREDIT CARD - A card that lets you buy things using borrowed money, which must be paid back with interest.

DEBIT CARD - A card that lets you buy things using money already deposited into a bank account.

DIRECT DEBIT - When a bank automatically pays a debt or deposits your money into a saving account.

DIVIDEND - A payment made to a shareholder by its company. The amount depends upon the company's profits. It is up to the company as dividends are not mandatory.

EQUITY - The value of something minus the money still owed to buy it. In terms of property, the equity equals the value of the property minus the mortgage.

EXPENSE - The cost of something or something you have to spend money on.

GROSS - The amount paid before tax is deducted.

INFLATION - The cost of living.

INTEREST - An amount of money paid for the use of money that is borrowed or invested.

INVESTMENT - Purchase of stocks, bonds, mutual fund shares, real estate and collectible annuities, with the expectation of obtaining income or capital gain in the future.

JOINT ACCOUNT - A bank or other account owned by multiple people.

LEGAL TENDER - Banknotes or coins which by law must be accepted as payment of a debt, or for a product or service; the currency of exchange, notes and coin, in a particular country.

LIABILITY - Debts or assets and investments that lose value rather than increase.

LIMITED ACCESS ACCOUNT - A saving account that will only let you withdraw money a few times annually.

LIQUID ASSET - An asset that can be traded into cash.

MINIMUM PAYMENT - The smallest amount you can pay monthly or annually for a debt.

MORTGAGE - A loan used to buy a home. There are several types of mortgages, each with its own terms and conditions.

NATIONAL SAVINGS AND INVESTMENTS - A savings account the government offer in which your money grows tax-free.

NEGATIVE EQUITY - When the value of an asset is worth less than the loan used to buy it.

NET - The amount paid after tax and any other deductions.

PATENT - A government licence giving someone the sole right to make, use or sell an invention for a set period.

PHILANTROPIST - The practice of helping people less well off than oneself and the love of mankind in general.

RECESSION - A period of time in the economic cycle when the economy is contracting rather than expanding.

SHARE OR STOCK - An investment in which you buy a portion of a company and can receive some of the company's profits. The amount you will receive depends on how big your share is.

STAGFLATION – Prices are rising but the economy is not growing.

STOCK EXCHANGE - Organised market place in which members of the exchange trade stocks, common stock equivalents, and bonds, acting both as agents (brokers) and as principles (dealers or traders). Such exchanges have a physical location where brokers and dealers meet to execute orders from institutional and individual investors to buy and sell securities.

STRUCTURING – The process by which money is broken into smaller amounts to avoid suspicion.

TERM - The length of time a borrower has to repay a loan.

The following are words more commonly used on the streets and are useful for any hustler.

BALLER - Originally someone who made money from sport but now the money can be made anyhow.

BELLY - A large amount of money.

BOX - A kilo of drugs.

BRICK - A kilo of drugs.

BUMP/KNOCK - To bump/knock someone is to dishonestly make money off them. It could be you sold them something fake or overcharged them.

CAKE - Originally a kilo of drugs; now also means money. If someone is caking they are making a lot.

CERTIFIED - Someone or something that is accepted as real.

CONNECT - Someone who can get you what you need at a good price.

DRINK - This is the extra money a middleman makes.

FLIPPING - Making money with money.

FLOSSING - Showing off what you have got.

FRONTER/STUNTER - A show off. Fronting or stunting means showing off.

GRINDING - Working hard.

LINE - A phone number used for business.

LINK - Someone who can get you something you need.

MOVE - Something you do to make money; also to sell something.

PUSHER/WORKER - An individual who sells drugs or other things for someone.

SHOTTA - Drug dealer. A shoot is someone who wants to buy something. Top shotta is the boss.

SQUARE - Credit or debit card.

STACK - Cash savings. Stacking is saving cash.

TICK - To borrow; it could be money or drugs. It means you will pay at a later date sometimes with interest.

TIGHT - A person who is scared to spend money. They are selfish and greedy.

TRAPHOUSE - House where drugs are chopped, mixed, cooked, bagged and sold.

TRAPPER - A hustler or shotta; a person who makes money from drugs.

WASH - To wash money means you are cleaning dirty (illegal) money; washing is also known as laundering.

MONEY SYMBOLS

Money symbols are subject to change as empires rise and fall.

Ar Ariary (Madagascar) ₳ Austral (Argentina)

฿ Baht (Thailand)

B/. Balboa (Panama) Br Birr (Ethiopia)

₿ Bitcoin (Global)

Bs. Bolivar/Boliviano (Venezuela) (Bolivia)

₵ Cedi (Guana)

₡ Colon (Costa Rica) ₢ Cruzeiro (Brasil)

D Dalasi (Gambia) Ден Denar (Macedonia)

دج Dinar (Algeria) .ب.د Dinar (Bahrain)

د.ع Dinar (Iraq) JD Dinar (Jordan)

د.ك Dinar (Kuwait)   د.ل Dinar (Libya)

Дин Dinar (Serbia)   د.ت Dinar (Tunisia)

د.م. Dirham (Morocco)

د.إ Dirham (United Arab Emirates)

$ Dollar (United States) (Antigua) (Australia)
(Bahamas) (Barbados) (Belize) (Bermuda) (Brunei)
(Canada) (Cayman Islands) (Dominica) (East Timor)
(Ecuador) (El Salvador) (Fiji) (Grenada) (Guyana)
(Hong Kong) (Jamaica) (Kirbati) (Liberia) (Marshal
Islands) (Federal States of Micronesia) (Namibia)
(Nauru) (New Zealand) (Palau) (Saint Kitts and
Nevis) (Saint Lucia) (Saint Vincint and Grenadines)
(Singapore) (Soloman Islands) (Suriname) (Taiwan)
(Trinidad and Tobago) (Tavalu) (Zimbabwe)

₫ Dong (Viatnam) ֏ Dram (Armenia)

Esc Escudo (Cape Verdean)

€ Euro (Austria) (Belgium) (Cyprus) (Estonia) (Finland) (France) (Germany) (Greece) (Ireland) (Italy) (Latvia) (Lithuania) (Luxembourg) (Malta) (Netherlands) (Portugal) (Slavakia) (Slovenia) (Spain)

f Florin (Aruba) Ft Forint (Hungary)

F Franc (France) (Benin) (Berkina Faso) (Burundi) (Cameroon) (Central African Republic) (Chad) (Republic of the Congo) (Democratic Republic of the Congo) (Comoros) (Cote d'lvoire) (Djibouti) (Equatorial Guinea) (Gabon) (Guinea) (Guinea-Bissau) (Liechtenstein) (Mali) (Niger) (Rwanda) (Senegal) (Switzerland) (Togo)

G Gourde (Haiti) ₲ Guarani (Paraguay)

h Haler (Czech Republic) Ħ Hus (Global)

₭ Kip (Laos)

Kr Krones/Krona (Denmark) (Faroe Islands) (Iceland) (Norway) (Sweden)

Kn Kuna (Croatia) MK Kwacha (Zambia)

K Kyat/Kinar (Burma) (Papua New Guinea)

L Lek (Albania)

Le Leone (Sierra Leone)

ЛВ Lev (Bulgaria)

E Lilangeni (Swaziland) £Lira (Turkey)

⋀ Manat (Azerbaijan) m Mill (Cyprus) (Malta)

₦ Naira (Nigeria) Nu. Ngultrum (Bhutan)

UM Ouguiya (Mauritania)

MOP$ Pataca (Macau)

S/. Peruvian Nuevo Sol (Peru)

Pts Peseta (Spain)

₱ Peso (Argentina) (Chile) (Colombia) (Cuba) (Dominican Republic) (Mexico) (Philippines) (Uruguay)

£ Pound (United Kingdom) (Egypt) (Falkland Islands) (Gibraltar) (Lebanon) (Manx) (South Sudan) (St. Helena) (Sudan) (Syria)

R$ Real (Brazil) ريال Rial (Iran)

ر.ع. Rial (Oman) ق.ر Rial (Qatar)

ر.س Rihal (Saudi Arabia)

RM Ringgit (Malaysia) ₽ Ruble (Russia)

Rf. Rufiyaa (Maldives) ₹ Rupee (India)

Rs Rupee (Mauritius) (Nepal) (Sri Lanka) (Pakistan)

₪ Shekel (Israel) Ksh Shilling (Kenya)

Sh.So. Shilling (Somalia)

USh Shilling (Uganda)

৳ Taka (Bangladesh)

WS$ Tala (Samoa)

₸ Tenge (Kazakhstan) ₮ Tugrik (Mongolia)

VT Vatu (Vanuata)

₩ Won (North Korea) (South Korea)

¥ Yen/Yuan (Japan) (China)

zł Zloty (Poland)

¤ Represents all symbols (Global)

CHAPTER 26

WORDS OF WISDOM

Throughout the history of language, different sayings, quotes and proverbs that relate to hustling, have emerged. Some are so great they leave an everlasting impact on the mind and like poetry they inspire thoughts and provoke ideas.

One of the most famous sayings is,

'Money can't buy happiness.'

The word happiness is only a word describing an emotion and so yes money cannot buy happiness but it can buy things that lead people to be happy. Usually,

'It is the lack of money that is the root of all evil.'

Where there is a lack, there is an unbalance. Greed, jealousy and envy can only exist when there is no balance. This unbalance can sometimes result in evil. The struggle and suffering can often lead to desperation and when a person is desperate they will often do things with no conscious mind. But

'Don't do the crime if you can't do the time.'

They say,

'Time is money',

But time is more precious than money. You can get money back but you cannot get time back. So decide what it is in life you value most.

'We know the price of everything but the value of nothing'.

If

'The best things in life are free',

Maybe the worst things in life come at a cost. Learning to cut costs and minimise expenses is part of being a hustler. Being able to budget and prioritise what is important to you will help you to manage your money but

'If you cannot control your money, your money will control you',

And

'If you cannot control your emotions, you cannot control your money.'

So learning self-control is essential. Learning how to manage yourself is essential. If you cannot manage yourself you will not be able to manage business.

'Business is like a car, it won't run itself except downhill',

So

'Value your money, don't just count it.'

Everyone's value will differ;

'One man's junk is another man's treasure',

And feeling rich is the first step to becoming rich.

'Success doesn't lead to happiness. Happiness leads to success.'

A wise man once said,

'The less you want, the richer you are.'

Appreciate what you have already so that you may appreciate more what you hustle for. Many people will do whatever it takes to get to what they believe is the top. With money comes politics:

'Steal a little and they throw you in jail, steal a lot and they make you king',

But remember,

'When the game is over, the pawn and the king go back in the same box.'

When stripped of material possessions and wealth you are just a human being. To be humble is to be wise.

'A fool who thinks he is a fool is for that reason a wise man. The fool who thinks that he is wise is called a fool indeed.'

These words of wisdom may inspire you to pursue your dreams but follow your own dreams and not somebody else's.

'Wisdom can come at any age; even an old man can be a fool',

So hustle with an open mind and open eyes.

'He who dares, wins.'

Have faith;

'Where there is no risk, there is no reward.'

You can only try your best in life but that is okay because

'God loves a trier.'

EPILOGUE

The word '*holy*' means morally and spiritually good. The true spirit and essence of a hustler comes to some people naturally and others need a manual. Just as it is with religion some people take their books literally, and others may use the scriptures more like guidelines, or a story that they can base things around. Find yourself and find your own faith. Discover the spirit inside. Be aware and respectful of others. Do not follow blindly. Follow your heart. Hustling is a religion, a way of life, a way to survive in the world. It is important not to lose your sense of self along the way. This means to be a true hustler you must be holy. Some people can go their entire life never picking up a book or following any gurus or spiritual leaders and still live a very balanced and pure life. This is becoming a lot harder. The knowledge in this book should be used for the sole purpose of bettering oneself whilst maintaining balance. Make money, be successful but always go back to your true essence. Remember what it is you value most. Consider what your priorities are. What makes you feel good, and what is actually good for you, might not be the same thing. Life is a journey. Remain conscious at all times. Awareness is vital in order to stay ahead yet being ahead might not make you as humble as you would like. Balance is the key to a healthy life. Health and freedom is wealth and a true hustler always strives to gain more wealth, and so maybe the journey is not actually about money but about hustling for freedom and health. There is no right or wrong. What is right for you may be wrong for someone else. The world and universe works with a balance that cannot be measured. There are some questions that remain unanswered and people have to have faith in the unknown. Balance in the world needs to be seen and felt; there is good and evil, rich and poor, happiness and suffering. Understand that certain methods of making money might make you richer and put a smile on your face but could make someone else poorer and subjected to pain. Could you live with this? Do not believe the money myths; that money is evil and corrupt. It is only those who use it in an evil way or those that would do terrible things to get hold of it that are evil. Money is just money and man is merely man. There are so many different conspiracies but do not let that put you off because that could be the real conspiracy; a group of elite who do not want the average man to prosper. The knowledge you have gained from this book should be used wisely to better yourself. Poverty is not only a lack of wealth but it is a lack of wealth of knowledge. Nothing can stop you from achieving your dreams but yourself, your ambition and your belief. Believe you have what it takes. Visualise yourself achieving your dreams. Thoughts are powerful and it is not a secret that thoughts manifest into reality. You can create your destiny but you cannot just dream. Do not dream about the things you wish to do. Do the things you dream about. Live your dreams. Be active and seek out the treasures of life. Continue to hustle and follow the rules, the guidelines, the true path and *The Hustler's Holy Book.* May you always meet with success. And remember...

GOD LOVES A HUSTLER

Printed in Great Britain
by Amazon